Dear Friends,

Our intrepid cousins usually choose to investigate suspicious circumstances on their own. Occasionally their activities intersect with law enforcement...but in this story, the tables are turned when Trooper Dan Benson needs Elaine and Jan to unofficially help him clear his best friend's name. At the same time, the cousins have family excitement of several kinds occurring. All these things occur against the backdrop of autumn in central Maine, a magical time of crisp temperatures, twilit evenings and the brilliant colors of leaves as the trees prepare for their winter naps.

Pumpkin recipes, apple cider, corn mazes...I love autumn and harvest festivals! A local museum near my childhood home has a pumpkin catapult that tosses pumpkins clear across a wide field during their annual harvest celebration, a ritual which never fails to delight the young-at-heart. The same museum has year-round exhibits sharing the reality of life in late eighteenth and early nineteenth century Pennsylvania, where nearly everything was grown or made on one's own property. Quilts and needlework of the original landowning family are displayed inside the large stone home. I love needle arts and have always enjoyed seeing these precious treasures stitched by loving hands nearly two centuries before I lived. In this story, Elaine and Jan host a quilting bee at Tea for Two, an event I enjoyed writing so much I wish I could have attended it myself!

This will be my last story for the Tearoom Mysteries series. Thank you for inviting me and my fellow authors into your homes and your imaginations.

Warmly,
Anne Marie Rodgers

Tearoom Mysteries

Tearoom for Two
Tea Rose
To a Tea
Crosswords and Chamomile
Burning Secrets
O Christmas Tea
On Thin Ice
Tea Is for Treasure
Trouble Brewing
Mystery and Macarons
The Tea Will Tell
Tea and Touchdowns
Steeped in Secrets
Stealing Santa
A Monumental Mystery
Whispers from the Past
Tearoom in a Tempest
Brimming with Questions
Beneath the Surface
Apart at the Seams
Turning the Tables

Turning the Tables

ANNE MARIE RODGERS

Guideposts
New York

Tearoom Mysteries is a trademark of Guideposts

Published by Guideposts Books & Inspirational Media
110 William Street
New York, New York 10038
Guideposts.org

Copyright © 2018 by Guideposts. All rights reserved.

This book, or parts thereof, may not be reproduced, stored in a retrieval system, or transmitted in any form or by any means, electronic, mechanical, photocopying, recording or otherwise, without the written permission of the publisher.

The characters and events in this book are fictional, and any resemblance to actual persons or events is coincidental.

Acknowledgments

Every attempt has been made to credit the sources of copyrighted material used in this book. If any such acknowledgment has been inadvertently omitted or miscredited, receipt of such information would be appreciated.

Scripture references are from the following sources: *The Holy Bible,* King James Version (KJV). *The Holy Bible, New International Version.* Copyright ©1973, 1978, 1984, 2011 by Biblica, Inc. Used by permission of Zondervan. All rights reserved worldwide. www.zondervan.com

Cover and interior design by Müllerhaus
Cover illustration by Ross Jones, represented by Deborah Wolfe, Ltd.
Typeset by Aptara, Inc.

Printed and bound in the United States of America
10 9 8 7 6 5 4 3 2 1

Turning the Tables

CHAPTER ONE

"Oh, look. The house across the street is going up for sale," Jan Blake observed.

Elaine Cook paused in the midst of dusting a drop-leaf half table in the east parlor of Tea for Two, the Victorian tearoom in central Maine that she co-owned with Jan. The widowed cousins had purchased the tearoom together a few years earlier when Elaine had returned to central Maine following her husband's passing. Her short, dark hair webbed with silver, Elaine wore a taupe twinset and matching flats paired with a forest-green pencil skirt, but she'd tossed a large white apron over her clothing for the cleaning portion of her day.

Her cousin Jan, conversely, had already removed hers because it was covered with flour. There also was still a spot of flour near one temple in her sleek dark hair. Jan had been in the kitchen for several hours earlier that morning, working her baking magic for the day's customers. Dressed in khakis, comfortable burlap Toms, and a tailored white blouse with three-quarter-length sleeves, the shorter woman had been kneeling on the chintz cushion of the window seat cleaning the bay windows at the front of the room, but she had paused for a moment, a faded rag and a spray bottle motionless in her hands as she stared out the window.

"The Battie house?" Elaine moved to join Jan at the window and pulled aside one panel of the lace curtain. She narrowed her blue eyes at the bright autumn sunshine outside.

Jan nodded. Her eyes, nearly the same blue as her cousin's, glowed with interest. There was an old Victorian across the street from theirs. A woman in a russet suit with a scarf in the shades of an autumn forest knotted at her neck had just finished pounding a For Sale sign into the leaf-littered grass of the front yard with a rubber mallet. As October marched on, the lawn wore an increasingly thick covering of fallen leaves.

"Hey, isn't that Sharon Reddick?" Sharon was the Realtor who had guided them through the process of buying their own home/business.

"Looks like it," Jan said. "She must have gotten the listing."

"I did tell Mrs. Battie what a good job she did for us," Elaine said. Mrs. Battie was the woman who owned the home across the street, though she spent almost all of her time in Florida, and had hardly been in town since they'd opened the tearoom. Still, when they were still looking at the house that would become the tearoom, Mrs. Battie had come over to meet them. When she'd decided to sell the house, she called Elaine from Florida to ask if she had a Realtor recommendation.

When she'd returned to the small SUV she had parked at the curb, the Realtor put away the mallet she'd been wielding and picked up a sheaf of papers. It took her only a moment to load those into a covered acrylic box attached to the sign.

"I might go grab a set of those specs," Jan said as the woman climbed into her vehicle and drove off. "I've been curious about that house for ages."

The Victorian was similar to theirs, although it looked smaller, and had stood empty for some time, although routine visits from a landscaping service and a cleaning company indicated that it was being kept up. The cousins and many of the locals who patronized the tearoom frequently wondered if their former neighbor intended to sell it at some point, but no one knew. Until now.

"Oh, look, there's already a notice about an open house." Elaine loved exploring the interiors of homes for sale. Even when she wasn't in the market—which she frequently had been during her husband's years as a career military officer—she still enjoyed viewing layouts and imagining how a home could be improved.

"We should go to it," Jan said.

"I'm surprised they'd do that right off the bat," Elaine said. "Usually they only host an open house right away if an owner wants a quick sale, or if the Realtor is having trouble moving a house." She pursed her mouth. "Then again, Mrs. Battie may be eager to unload it."

"Speaking of hosting," Jan said, as Elaine let the lace curtain slip back into place and returned to her task, "we need to review our plans for the Autumn Tea."

The cousins had decided to plan a special fall-themed day for the tearoom. They had found that customers, particularly the locals who came in regularly, loved unusual activities. Invariably, the tearoom was quickly booked solid when they announced a special event.

Elaine smiled. "I guess that's coming up soon. I can't believe we're this far into October." They had planned the Autumn Tea for the latter half of the month. Their special event would feature a quilting bee to complete a harvest-themed quilt that would be auctioned off for charity at the Chickadee Lake Harvest Home Festival.

"I can't wait for the quilting bee," Elaine said. "Even though I don't quilt, I think it's going to be such fun."

"You still can join us," Jan assured her. "We already have enough experienced quilters signed up. I want to encourage anyone who's interested, even if they don't know how to quilt. We'll have our veterans teach anyone who's new to hand-quilting."

"It almost makes me want to try," Elaine said, grinning. "But I'll help Rose and Archie with the tearoom duties that day so that you can focus on the quilting project." Rose Young and Archie Bentham were the cousins' two employees.

"Camille Lapole called me yesterday to ask how the quilt blocks were coming along," Jan told her cousin. Camille was a friend of Jan's who was a highly experienced quilter. In exchange for a cake for her daughter's upcoming wedding, she had agreed to supervise the quilt project and help with both the morning and afternoon sessions. She had chosen six complementary fabrics, and between her and Jan, they had recruited quilters to piece thirty harvest-themed appliquéd quilt blocks. The quilters could choose to create a design of their own or take a precut package with instructions for a specific block.

"Isn't the deadline for completing the blocks tomorrow?" Elaine asked. When Jan nodded, Elaine said, "And have you received them all?"

"Not all," Jan admitted, "but most of them. I've got a few calls to make."

"Sounds like you're in good shape though. I ordered the tea we chose yesterday. Have you decided what types of baked goods you want to offer?"

"Tell me about the tea again," Jan said as she finished washing the final window pane. "Apple something?"

"Harvest Apple," Elaine corrected. "It's a red rooibos made with bits of sweet dried apple, autumn spices, nettle leaf, and sunflower petals. It's billed as 'delicious and full-bodied,' according to the Winterwoods Tea Company in Spokane. We've gotten some wonderful products from them before, so I'm confident that this will be tasty."

"It sounds perfect for our autumn celebration," Jan said. "Apples and sunflowers—we can use those as decorating themes, along with pumpkins, gourds, mums, miniature hay bales, and Indian corn." Her eyes sparkled. "I'm excited already."

"What will we serve?" Elaine prompted.

Jan thought for a minute. "How about your mother's pumpkin loaf recipe? It's so beautiful when it's sliced."

"Oh, that's a great idea," Elaine said, thinking of the pretty pinwheel look of the loaf. "And won't Mom be thrilled? We can call it 'Grandma's Pumpkin Roll.'" Her mother, Virginia Willard, had a family recipe that called for a thin layer of pumpkin loaf baked in a jelly roll pan that was rolled up and left to cool while a cream cheese mixture was whipped up. It was then unrolled and spread with the mixture, rolled up again, secured in plastic wrap, and refrigerated or frozen. When the cold roll was sliced, the result was a gorgeous spiral effect, and the taste was so sweetly divine few people could eat more than one slice.

"Along with that," Jan said, "I saw a lovely recipe for puff pastry apple blossoms, and for the chocolate-lovers, a chocolate pecan pie."

Elaine pressed a hand to her stomach. "I'm salivating already. And oh, the decorating ideas! I can hardly wait."

"*I* can hardly wait to see the finished quilt," Jan said. "Those autumn batiks Camille chose are beautiful, and the quilt blocks that have been turned in so far are absolutely stunning. I keep wanting to lay them out and start trying to arrange them, but until we have them all—and until I finish my own—there's no point. We could have it all tentatively arranged and then have to change it if the last one doesn't work in the space left."

Elaine laughed, picking up on the one memorable detail in Jan's words. "The deadline's tomorrow and you're not done with your own?"

"It'll be done before it's needed," Jan said primly, grinning.

"Good morning." A new voice intruded on their merriment. "I've started boiling water since it's nearly time to open. Jan, is there anything special you'd like me to work on today?"

Both cousins turned to greet Rose Young. The young woman had started as a server, but since she'd begun attending culinary school, she had become Jan's invaluable pastry assistant. Her flaxen hair was twisted into a charming up-do this morning, and she already had donned a white chef's coat over her black trousers and blouse.

"Good morning, Rose. I made cream puffs this morning, and I imagine they're cool now. The filling already is made and is in the refrigerator if you want to start with them. We also need to make the ham, brie, and apple crustless sandwiches and whip up some tomato-cheddar on wheat. And just for something different, I made a small selection of spinach and artichoke puff pastries. Recently we've had several people asking for pastries that are less sweet, so I thought we'd try them."

"Yum. I'll be your taste-tester." Rose grinned, winking one blue eye.

As the pair headed for the kitchen, Elaine walked through the parlors to ensure everything was in place for the day. She filled several sugar bowls and brought fresh napkins up front so they'd be able to quickly bus and freshen tables.

Then she unlocked the front door, turned over the Closed sign to read Open, and began to sweep off the porch and front steps.

Earl Grey, the resident cat who had adopted them and who lived more or less on their back porch year round—and in a protected shelter during the worst of the winter weather—joined her, his furry tail a stately plume held high above his back as he stalked the broom.

An SUV bearing the markings of the Maine State Police pulled to a stop along the curb, and Trooper Dan Benson's tall frame slowly emerged. "Morning, Elaine." Dan and his family were members of the church she and Jan attended, and since the tearoom had opened, they had worked with him several times in their pursuit of unraveling a mystery. To Dan's exasperation, their methods were not always as straightforward as his, although she rather thought he had grown to respect their abilities.

"Good morning, Dan," she said cheerfully. "Beautiful day, isn't it?"

"It is," he agreed. The sky was clear. Under the morning sun warming the chilly autumn air, Dan's buzz-cut blond hair gleamed as he nodded, confirming his agreement. "Do you think Jan would consider making me a few sandwiches and wrapping up a pastry or two to go this morning? I have to drive over east to Ellsworth for an investigation today, and I'm afraid I'm going to get stuck in the car without lunch."

Elaine chuckled, setting aside the broom. "I'm sure she will. Come on in."

Dan followed her into the foyer, carrying his Stetson uniform hat as he did so. Together they walked back to the kitchen.

"Well, look what the wind blew in," Jan said when she saw him. "Good morning." She had turned on the small kitchen television already, and she reached over and grabbed the remote to lower the volume.

"Good morning." Dan lifted his face slightly and sniffed. "It smells terrific in here. What are you making?"

"I knew you didn't just stop by to say hello," Jan teased before giving him a rundown of their daily specials. "What can we get you?"

Dan grinned. "You caught me." He told her what he'd told Elaine about his day's travels. "I was hoping maybe you could make me a couple of sandwiches of whatever you've got. That ham-brie-apple one sounded fantastic. But you don't have to trim the crusts off mine," he added hastily.

Elaine couldn't prevent a snicker. "We wouldn't want your fellow troopers to see you eating sandwiches that didn't look manly." Rose and Jan both laughed, and Dan looked sheepish.

"You said it, I didn't," he pointed out. "But you might be right."

They all chuckled again.

"Will you need a drink?" Elaine asked.

Dan shook his head. "I have a supersized insulated mug of coffee in the cruiser."

As Jan's nimble hands began to assemble his sandwiches, Dan said, "So what are you two up to these days? Any new investigations you need help with?"

"Nothing urgent," Elaine told him, gratified that he did indeed appreciate their penchant for solving mysteries.

"We'd be happy to help you out if you have any investigations *you* need help with," Jan told him, turning his offer back on him.

Dan grinned. "We have nothing I can divulge to civilians, but I appreciate the offer."

Jan's cell phone rang then, and she excused herself to answer it. Rose stepped in to finish putting Dan's sandwiches together while Elaine bagged some of the pastries.

A moment later, Jan stepped back into the kitchen, looking concerned.

"Problem?" Elaine queried.

"Possibly," Jan said. "That was one of the other members of the Chickadee Lake Harvest Home Festival committee. We have to hold an emergency meeting Saturday afternoon. Apparently the committee chairman, Hester Ronsard, has met with an accident."

"Oh no. What happened?"

"I don't know," Jan said slowly. "Eulalie didn't have any details. She was just part of a phone tree started by someone else."

"Ronsard," Dan said. "I heard an emergency call go out last night, and I'm pretty sure I heard that name. Does she live near the other end of the lake?"

Jan nodded. "Yes, just outside Penzance."

"I believe someone fell down a flight of stairs," Dan said. "There may have been broken bones and/or a head injury involved. Sorry, I wasn't listening closely. I do know the injured person was transported to the hospital."

"Oh dear, that doesn't sound good." Jan bit her lip. "The festival is just over two weeks away, and we have a lot of details to finalize."

"I'll add Hester to my prayer list," Elaine said. "I really hope she wasn't badly hurt."

Dan's cell phone rang then, and he pulled it from his pocket. Smiling, he thumbed it on, turned away and said, "Hey, honey, what's up?" Then his body stiffened, and he listened intently. "What? No way...No way! Who told you the police talked to him? Hold on." He turned to the cousins and Rose and said, "Excuse me, please," before disappearing into the front of the house.

Elaine frowned. "Sounds like a friend of Dan's must be in trouble."

"Maybe we'd better add Dan to our prayer lists too," Jan said, before they lapsed into an uneasy silence.

Moments later, Dan returned to the kitchen. Rose had finished building his sandwiches, and Jan was bagging them. "Would you please grab a couple of our disposable napkins?" she asked Rose. As Rose entered the pantry, Jan said, "Everything okay?" to Dan.

The trooper shook his head. "Not at all. I just heard that a friend is in some difficulty—" He stopped suddenly, his gaze riveted on the TV.

Following the direction his eyes were looking, Jan quickly turned the volume up so they could hear. The local news team was breaking a story about a newly discovered theft and potential embezzlement from a statewide nonprofit called Homes for Maine Heroes headquartered in Waterville, just ten miles up the road from Lancaster.

HMH was a stellar organization that built specially modified homes for wounded soldiers and other local heroes like firefighters with polytrauma—multiple severe injuries sustained in one event. In some cases, HMH modified an existing home. HMH, the report went on, also provided Maine's heroes with special vehicles and mobility devices to make day-to-day living easier. Unfortunately, the nonprofit's chief executive officer, Alex DeRone, had been suspended on suspicion of theft and embezzlement, and charges were pending.

Dan's face had turned white.

"Dan," Elaine said gently, "is Alex DeRone the friend you were speaking of a moment ago?"

Dan nodded. "Yes."

"And you don't believe he's guilty?"

Dan shook his head. "He would never do that."

"You know him well?" Jan asked.

Dan exhaled heavily, his shoulders sagging. "He's been my buddy since I was five years old. We acted as best man in each other's weddings, and we're the godfathers for each other's kids."

Elaine let out a low whistle. "Wow. No wonder you don't believe he would commit a crime."

Dan smiled, but there was no amusement in it. "He wouldn't. Ever. Plus, he loves working for HMH. He would never do anything to harm that organization's reputation. Hearing that funds have been stolen from a nonprofit could make donors very leery of giving HMH more money." He shook his head. "Nope. Alex would never do that." He started for the door. "I have to talk to him."

"Dan, wait. Here's your lunch." Elaine grabbed his arm. "Take a deep breath. Maybe you can help get this straightened out, but you can't help him if you're this upset."

"You're right. You're right." He nodded, sucked in a deep breath, and blew it out again. "Thanks." He took the paper bag with his sandwiches and pastries that Jan held out and picked up his hat. "Put this on my tab and I'll catch it later."

"This one's on us," Jan told him, her eyes filled with sympathy. "We'll pray for your friend. Let us know if there's any way we can help."

Dan nodded. "Will do. Thank you." He sounded a little more like himself as he exited the kitchen.

The cousins listened to the trooper's footfalls as he strode across the foyer to the front door and let himself out.

"Well." Elaine shook her head. "I hope he's right about his buddy. He's going to be devastated if Alex DeRone really is the one who stole from Homes for Maine's Heroes."

CHAPTER TWO

Later the same evening, Jan and Elaine were relaxing in their private sitting room on the second floor working on projects while they half-watched a National Geographic Channel special about a human-like fossil that had been found in Africa two years ago.

Elaine was looking through a pile of children's catalogs she'd collected, considering getting a start on her Christmas gift ordering as she searched for an interesting present for her granddaughter, Lucy, whose twelfth birthday was approaching next month. Come to think of it, Lucy's brother Micah's ninth birthday was in January, so she ought to just get that out of the way while she was at it.

"What do you think of this?" Jan sat at the small game table, over which she had spread ribbon, some realistic-looking silk autumn leaves, and a few other decorative pieces she was using to dress up a large grapevine wreath. She held up a swath of brown-and-gold ribbon and several of the decorations. "Yes?"

"Very pretty," Elaine said. "But you could make something lovely out of just about anything. Your eye for color and design is such a gift."

"Thanks," Jan said as her cell phone, lying on the table to one side, rang. She glanced at the readout and her face lit up. "It's Amy," she said, referring to her middle child. She hit the button to open the call and said, "Hi, honey. Elaine's here with me, so I'm putting you on speaker."

"Hi, Mom. Hi, Elaine. How was business today?"

"Good," Jan said. "We're gearing up for our Autumn Tea. Remember I told you about the quilt squares?"

"Oh yes. That's such a great idea. I can't wait to see it."

"How are you feeling?" Amy was pregnant with her third child, and her early months had been plagued with exhaustion and occasional nausea.

"Not too bad." Amy sounded cautious, as though she was assessing her physical state at that particular moment. "And I didn't feel like I was going to die if I didn't get a nap this afternoon." She giggled. "At least, no more than non-pregnant me does."

Jan and Elaine both laughed.

"The Wednesday after next," Amy went on, "Van and I are going for another ultrasound. This is the one where we can learn the gender of the baby if we want."

"And do you want to?" Jan asked.

"Yes," Amy said immediately. "We can't wait. Oh, I hope it's a girl this time."

"We'll love either," Jan said, "but a little bundle of pink would be fun." Amy and Van already had twin sons.

"That's so exciting," Elaine said. "It still amazes me that you can find out the sex of your baby so long before you deliver."

"I'm excited to find out," Amy said, "but honestly, I think you got the easier deal. Now there's all this pressure to come up with a super-unique 'gender reveal' idea to post on Facebook." She sighed. "Mom, you forgot to give me your creative gene, so I'm going to need help figuring something out."

"I can do that. Do you have any theme or idea in mind?" Jan asked.

"I guess we have two choices," Amy said. "We could go with a fall theme since I'm going to be finding out on the Wednesday after next—"

"Oh, I just realized that's the day of the Autumn Tea," Jan said.

"Or we could do something spring-ish since that will be near my due date. So, pumpkins or spring showers and bunnies. Take your pick."

"Your baby. You pick," Jan said promptly.

Amy laughed. "All right. I guess fall, since it would just feel weird to decorate for spring in October. I saw some cute ideas on Pinterest and I pinned some I thought might be good starting points. Want me to send you the link?"

"Yes, please," Jan said. "That way, I'll have some idea of what appeals to you."

They chatted for a few more minutes before Amy suddenly yawned. "Uh-oh," she said. "The battery's dying. Mine, not my phone's." She chuckled. "Gotta head for bed soon."

With a laugh, Jan ended the call. She and Elaine smiled at each other. "I'm glad she's through the first trimester," Jan said. "And I'm excited about this gender-reveal. You're drafted to help me. We'll have to find something really special."

"It seems to me," Elaine said, "that since it's the day of the Autumn Tea, we ought to find some way to incorporate it right into our theme."

"Oh." Jan's eyes widened, and Elaine could see the ideas floating through her cousin's fertile imagination. "That's a terrific thought. Yes, we'll definitely have to work on that."

Companionable silence fell again. Elaine turned up the volume of the TV show she'd silenced when Amy called.

Jan soon finished her preliminary work on the wreath and carried the supplies back to her little sewing and craft room down the hall. Moments later, she returned with the quilt block she'd been piecing. "I need to finish this," she said, grinning. "If I'm going to be making phone calls this weekend to remind people to get theirs in, I can't be tardy myself."

Elaine smiled. "How much do you have to go?"

"Very little," Jan said. "I just need to embroider the rest of the piece of pumpkin vine and then I'll iron it one last time to set the stitches." She held up the block. "I'm pleased with it."

"I think it's gorgeous," Elaine said. Jan had sewn rust, rich brown, gold, and orange batik fabric squares into strips that she'd pieced together and placed on the diagonal. Then she'd cut the strips into sections and randomly pieced those to make a decent-size swatch of fabric. Once she had a large enough section completed, she cut the strips diagonally again the other way and sewed them together, creating a pumpkin composed of small diamonds that occupied most of her quilt square. She'd added a stem of a brown-striped fabric and a green-veined fabric leaf and was appliquéing the whole item to a background of pale rosy-gold batik that was intended to be the background theme for the quilt. She'd also embroidered a few stalks of grass at each side of the pumpkin's base, and a curling piece of pumpkin vine corkscrewing out from the stem. Elaine couldn't wait to see the completed effort. It was going to be stunning.

A few minutes later, Jan said, "I can't get Dan's bad news from this morning out of my head."

"I know." Elaine set down the pen she'd been using to make notes about gift ideas. "He seemed so certain his friend couldn't have stolen any money."

"It's not a trifling amount," Jan noted. "Didn't that news report say it was over twenty grand and probably much more?"

Elaine nodded. Then something occurred to her. "Hey, doesn't Penny Jillette work at HMH?" Penny was a fellow member of Lancaster Community Church. She and Jan had taken a sewing class together some years ago, and after Jan had invited her to visit LCC, Penny had joined and become an active member.

"Yes, she's in the Needlework Guild with me. I believe she works in public relations at HMH. Why?"

Elaine shrugged. "I was just thinking that she might be someone who would have some insights about what happened."

"Maybe," Jan said, "but how would we bring up the topic without sounding like a pair of nosy old ladies?"

ON FRIDAY, THE cousins and Archie Bentham, a British expat and tea connoisseur whose presence gave the tearoom a delightful feeling of authenticity, were cleaning up after the morning rush. It had been somewhat less frantic than summer's standard when tourists filled every table in both parlors, and they were nearly finished bussing tables when the front door opened, and Dan Benson entered the foyer.

"Hey there." Elaine set down the tray she'd been holding and headed toward him. "How are you doing? Any word on your friend?"

As she drew closer, she could see that he looked as despondent as she'd ever seen him. "Nothing helpful," he said, shaking his head and shrugging helplessly.

"Come on back to the kitchen," she said. "Sometimes it helps to talk things through." She gave Jan a tilt of her head to indicate that Jan should join them in the kitchen, and as she led the way to the back of the house, she saw Jan step over to speak to Archie, who would easily be able to handle the tables still seated.

Rose was not coming in today, so there was no one in the kitchen. Elaine indicated their small kitchen table. "Have a seat. Want some tea?"

"Sure. Something with caffeine if you've got it."

Elaine smiled. Working quickly, she chose a British black tea with the highest caffeine content they had. Instead of a china cup and saucer, she took down one of her own large mugs from the cupboard. While the tea steeped, she cut one of Jan's still-warm blueberry muffins into quarters and arranged them on a flowered Royal Albert china plate, just as Jan came through the door from the hall.

After she poured Dan's tea, Elaine set the mug and the food before him with a fork and napkin. "Here you go. Caffeine and pastry. Just what the doctor ordered."

Dan smiled slightly as he took a drink, but the expression faded as quickly as it began, leaving his blue eyes serious and melancholy. "I don't know how to help my buddy Alex," he said. "I hate feeling so helpless."

Jan pulled out a chair and took a seat across from the trooper as Elaine sat at his right hand. "I thought you might be in a position to hear how the investigation's going, and maybe put in a good word for him," she said. "Isn't that the case?"

Dan shook his head. "The crime didn't originate in my jurisdiction, so it's not easy to get information about it. I did try late yesterday, but about all I heard was that it's an open-and-shut case." He looked utterly miserable.

"That's not good news," Jan said, sitting up straighter, "because if they are convinced he's the one who embezzled the money, then they're not going to be looking for whoever really did it."

"Right." Dan sighed.

"Why don't you tell us exactly what has happened so far?" Elaine suggested. "Everything you can think of."

Dan dropped his forehead into his hands, then scrubbed both palms back over his hair before dropping them dispiritedly to the table. "He was arrested for theft last night, but further charges are pending. Embezzlement, I'm sure, which is much more serious than simple theft. He's out on bail right now, but as you heard yesterday, he was suspended from Homes for Maine's Heroes, so he's just sitting around the house staring at the walls and going crazy while the investigators comb through his finances and those of HMH. I called him last night, but I can't visit without a good reason. The last thing either of us needs is for the investigation to get muddled because of his relationship with a state trooper."

"And you're still certain he didn't have anything to do with it?" Elaine asked.

Dan nodded. "I'd stake my life on it if I were a betting man. He's been my best friend for years. I know him as well as I know my own family. Alex would never, ever steal money, especially from a wounded warriors' organization."

"What will happen if he's found guilty?" Jan asked.

"It depends," Dan said. "In Maine, penalties in embezzlement cases are based on the amount that was stolen. I'm sure they're trying to prove he embezzled more than ten grand, because then they can give him a big prison sentence as well as a fine."

"Prison!" Jan exclaimed. "For how long?"

Dan shrugged, taking another swallow of tea. "It depends. If the amount is over $10,000, he could get five to ten years in addition to a fine of twenty grand or even more if the judge is really tough."

Elaine sucked in a shocked breath. "That's...a lot. Both prison time and money."

Dan nodded. "Embezzlement is considered an especially heinous crime because, unlike simple larceny, which anyone can commit anywhere, an embezzler is in a position of trust within a company or with an individual. There is nothing impetuous or spontaneous about embezzlement. It takes forethought and planning."

"And you can't look into it at all?" Jan asked incredulously.

Dan shook his head. "It's not my case," he said unhappily. "Even if it was, I'd have to turn it over to someone else, since I have a personal relationship with the accused. And like I said, it's not my jurisdiction, so I can't even inquire without raising red flags. If I meddle in any way or try to insist that I know he's innocent, it could make Alex look guiltier and undermine any credibility he might have. But I know he didn't do it," he added fiercely, his hands clenched on the table. "I know it."

"Dan." Elaine's voice was serious, and Jan looked over at her alertly. "Could we look into it for you?" Her eyes met Jan's. "We realized last night we know someone who works at HMH, and we may be able to get more information for you. In fact, you may know her too, or at least be acquainted with her in passing. She goes to our church."

Dan raised his gaze from the table, his expression unreadable. "Who is it?"

"Penny Jillette."

"She works in public relations at HMH," Jan told him. "I met her some years ago and invited her to church. She joined shortly after that. I bet Charlotte knows her. Isn't she in the Needlework Guild?"

Dan nodded. "I know her. Not well, but to speak to. And yes, my wife's spoken of her many times." A spark of what could only be hope lit his eyes, and he grinned, shaking his head. "I never thought I'd be asking you to do this, but would you be willing to apply your investigative skills to help Alex out of this mess?"

The cousins looked at each other, telegraphing assent, before Jan looked across the table at Dan. "We'd be happy to."

"Do you think," Elaine asked, "that we can speak with him directly?"

Dan nodded. "That's a good idea. Why don't you two come by my house on Monday around one? I'm sure he'd be willing to talk with you." His smile dimmed. "It's not like he has a lot of other things to do."

"Will it cause trouble for you to have him come to your house?"

"I think one visit will be okay. We can always say we already had plans to get together that day if anyone happens to notice and question him. But that will be it. I really can't be seen with him after Monday."

CHAPTER THREE

Friday had gotten busy and stayed that way after Dan's visit, so it wasn't until that evening that Jan had time to count all the quilt blocks that had been turned in and check them off her list. Two women had brought theirs in that day, which meant that there were only two blocks outstanding.

On Saturday morning, after she'd finished her early baking, her morning devotionals, and her breakfast, she made calls to the two women who had yet to turn in their blocks. Both apologized. One promised to bring hers by the tearoom that day, while the other, who attended Lancaster Community Church, said she'd bring it with her tomorrow.

That afternoon, Elaine took over the rest of the workday so that Jan could attend the emergency meeting of the Chickadee Lake Harvest Home Festival committee that had been called in the wake of the chairman's accident. The meeting was held in the parish hall of a small church in Penzance.

Jan was the fourth person to enter the little stone building and make her way through a short hallway to the adjacent fellowship hall. Two others were right behind her, which meant everyone was there—everyone, of course, except their seventh member and chairman, Hester Ronsard, the unfortunate accident victim.

"Hi, Jan." Pearl Trexler, who also attended Lancaster Community Church with her husband, Will, pulled out a chair, which Jan slid into. "I heard Hester's out of commission for a while," Pearl whispered.

"Who's taking over the committee?" Jan asked.

Pearl shrugged. "I think we need to decide that today."

After everyone was seated, Alvin Shoetter rose to his feet. Alvin was a tall, thin man who taught history at Forest High. "Thank you for coming on such short notice, everyone," he said. His Adam's apple bobbed. "As you may have heard, Hester fell down her basement steps on Thursday. Her husband called me to let me know someone was going to have to take over the festival committee, and I promptly activated a phone chain to call this meeting. Unfortunately, Hester sustained a head injury as well as breaking her left leg in two places. She is currently hospitalized and obviously will not be able to continue in her role as chair of the committee. I picked up her notebook and files from her husband this morning." He indicated a tote bag at one side of the table. "Now." He cleared his throat nervously. "Is anyone able to step up and take this on? I'm chairing the woodcarving, pumpkin catapult, and logrolling events, and I'm barely managing to keep track of that, so I'm out."

"Not me," said Eulalie Watson promptly. A solidly built soccer coach who had worked with a local children's team for years, she was the one who had called Jan after the accident.

"I'm coordinating the talent show, which is practically a full-time job."

"Jan," said Pearl, "would you consider it? You have great organizational skills."

Jan looked reproachfully at her older friend. "What about you?"

"I'm managing the contests for the cakes, pies, jellies and jams, crochet and knitted projects, and the quilts, and I'm still getting new entries. I'm going to have to figure out how to accommodate larger-than-normal displays. I'm afraid if I try to juggle one more ball, I'll drop them all."

"I'll be gone all next week visiting family in Indiana," said Jim Beadle. Jim was a dairy farmer who appeared to be wearing the same overalls he'd had on since daybreak. "But I've got the sheep-shearing, the butter-churning, and the apple-cider pressing organized already. It's the same folks who did it in years past, so they pretty much know how to come in, set up, and do their thing."

"I'm working on the live music schedule and trying to get the historical displays organized," Jan said. "I really don't know—"

"We'll all try to help," Alvin said hastily. "Please, Jan?"

"I'm in charge of recruiting volunteers," said Dorothy Book. "I will get you anyone you need if you say yes." Dorothy was a real estate agent with a thriving business, but she still made time for a lot of community volunteerism. Jan knew if anyone could get her more volunteers, Dorothy could.

Jan smiled. "It doesn't sound as if I have a choice. But yes, I guess I can step in for Hester."

"Oh, thank you," Pearl said, and the rest of the committee echoed her.

Jan stood and went to pick up the bag Alvin had brought in. "I'm counting on each of you to have your own events organized as well, and I'll look through Hester's notes and see what still needs to be done."

"I think the only thing that isn't completely taken care of yet is the corn maze," Alvin told her. "No one on the committee ever signs up for that because the Chickadee Lake Boy Scout Troop always does it. I wouldn't worry about that. I'm sure it's taken care of."

Back at the tearoom, Elaine was just finishing emptying the dishwasher as Jan arrived. "How did your meeting go?" she asked. "How's Hester and who's taking over?"

Jan snorted. "I got railroaded. Shanghaied. Thrown to the wolves. Whatever uncomplimentary way you want to phrase it, I got suckered into chairing the committee in Hester's absence." She sobered. "Sounds like she took a really bad fall. Head injury and a badly broken leg. She's still in the hospital."

"Oh, that's terrible," Elaine said. "Maybe we can take her a meal once she's home. I'm sure her husband is going to have his hands full caring for her."

"Good idea." Jan slipped the tote bag of the chairman's notes off her shoulder and slung it onto one of the kitchen chairs. She sagged into another chair and sighed. "I can't believe I got stuck with this. Pearl Trexler threw me right under the bus."

"Better you than Pearl," Elaine said logically. "She's got more than a decade on you, and if I know Pearl, she's overextended already. Plus, you're so organized that you'll make this happen no matter what."

"I'm only doing it for the good of the team," Jan said. "They'd better not look at me next year."

Elaine chuckled. "You can always arrange to be out of town or something."

"That," said Jan, "might be one of the best ideas you've had in some time." Resigned to her fate, she started to haul the chairman's notebook out of the tote bag.

Elaine glanced at the time on the microwave. "Aren't you going out to dinner and that play in Waterville with Bob this evening?" Bob, a lawyer, was Jan's beau.

Jan leaped up. "I am! This will have to wait until tomorrow. See?" she said, dashing for the door. "I'm already behind."

ON SUNDAY MORNING, the cousins met in the vestibule after Sunday school ended. They had a few minutes before they needed to slip into their pew for the church service, so they craned their necks, scanning the gathering congregants for Penny Jillette.

"Did you see her yet?" Jan asked.

Elaine shook her head. "No. She doesn't usually get here too far ahead of time." They both took another moment to look around at the people pouring into their little white clapboard house of worship. "Remember, we have to be careful what we say about Homes for Maine's Heroes," Elaine said. "We don't want to give any impression that we're investigating the theft."

"So how are we going to get her to talk about it?" Jan asked, ever practical.

Elaine grinned. "I don't know, but something will occur to me. Penny! Hi!" She waved over Jan's shoulder. "How have you been?"

"Great. Hi, Elaine, hi, Jan. How are you?" Penny was petite and green-eyed, with improbably bright red hair and liberally sprinkled freckles. Elaine always thought she looked like a particularly adorable lady leprechaun.

"Hi, Penny," Jan said as she turned to greet the younger woman. "I'm fine. Are you planning on entering any of your needlework in the Harvest Home Festival contest? I always love seeing your use of color in your quilting."

"Thanks. I could say the same to you. As it happens, I am thinking of entering an appliqué wall-hanging and a set of bargello place mats. I'm still finishing the place mats."

"Bargello pieces take forever." Jan shuddered theatrically. "All that aligning, pinning, and ironing. But the end result is lovely."

"Are you entering anything?" Penny asked.

Jan shook her head. "I've been too busy with Tea for Two this year to do any exhibition pieces. Plus, I'm on the organizing committee, so it would feel a little odd if I entered."

"Oh, that's silly," Penny said. "If you won, everyone would know it was on the merits of the piece. I hope you won't let that stop you."

"I really don't have anything to enter," Jan said. "Plus, I'm getting another grandbaby in the spring, so I am about to go into crazed knit-and-crochet mode."

"Congratulations," Penny said. "I hadn't heard. Things have been a little wild at work this week."

"You must mean the theft and embezzlement thing," said Elaine casually. "I thought of you when I saw HMH was involved. I hope it hasn't been too difficult."

"It's been awful. Just awful," Penny pronounced. Her eyes teared up a little. "My boss is such a kind, lovely man. We're all in complete shock that he's been arrested. We just can't believe he would do something like this."

"It's hard to imagine that someone in such a position of trust and authority would steal from his own company," Elaine said, recalling some of Dan's words.

"It is." Penny nodded, her distress evident. "It appears the evidence was extremely strong. Checks that should have been deposited the week prior were found hidden in his desk. Almost half a million dollars, if you can imagine that." Half a million?! The news report had said twenty thousand or more. Half a million was a whole different ball game. "He swears he didn't take any money," Penny continued, "but if he didn't, then who did? I guess the police will figure it all out eventually, but I am a little nervous about going in to the office tomorrow morning."

"I bet," Jan murmured.

"Oh, that reminds me," Penny said, "do either of you know anyone who might be willing to do a little volunteer work at HMH over the next two weeks? I have a short-term project putting photos from our first decade into chronological order and placing them in scrapbooks and PowerPoint presentations, and I'm looking for a volunteer or two. Someone with strong organizational skills would be great."

Jan's eyebrows rose. "I wish I could. I am going to be up to my ears in work between the tearoom and getting ready for the festival. Maybe Elaine could squeeze out some time."

"I could probably manage that," Elaine said, "if you think you, Rose, and Archie could keep things under control at Tea for Two." She looked at Jan, trying not to reveal her excitement at having the dilemma of how to get into the building solved so neatly.

Jan appeared to consider this, although Elaine knew she probably was dancing a jig inside as well. "Well, we're experiencing the fall tourist season, but it's definitely more manageable than high summer, so if you want to help out, I'd say sure thing."

Elaine smiled at Penny. "There you go. I'm at your service." She thought of tomorrow's late-lunch meeting with Alex DeRone. "Do you want me to start this week? I think I could come in for the first time on Tuesday, and I could probably give you some time each day after that."

"Oh, could you?" Penny's eyes sparkled. "That would be amazing. I'd love to get started on that project right away."

"You name the time, and I'll be there," Elaine promised.

"Come in around ten," Penny invited. "That will give me time to get myself organized."

Elaine gave her a thumbs-up. "Will do. See you then."

As Penny turned to greet another friend, the cousins looked at each other.

"That," Jan pronounced, "was a terrific stroke of luck."

"Or an answer to prayer," Elaine said. "What better way to investigate than to be right there at the scene of the crime?"

Emilee Sanders, a woman with white hair attractively coiffed, approached from the side. "Oh, Jan, I am so sorry. I forgot to bring my quilt block today! Can I get it to you one day this week?"

"Hi, Emilee," Jan said. "That's no problem. I could stop by right after church and pick it up if you like."

"Oh, that would be fine," the woman assured her. "I can't believe I forgot it. I'm really looking forward to the quilting bee on the day of your Autumn Tea. I love hand quilting."

"Great. I'll be counting on you to instruct some of our first-timers," Jan said with a smile.

Emilee nodded. "I'll be happy to help."

As she wandered away, Jan said, "That made me realize Sherry McClaren never brought hers by yesterday." She sighed. "I guess I'll have to call her again."

"Good morning, Mom. Hi, Jan." Elaine's daughter, Sasha, approached with her boyfriend at her side, and the cousins exchanged greetings with the couple. Sasha had moved to Lancaster from Colorado a few months ago after meeting and falling hard for Brody Samson, a handsome former soldier. The young couple recently had visited the church and had returned several times since. Elaine dared to dream that someday Sasha might join.

Hugging each of them, Sasha said, "How are you two? Sorry I haven't been by. It was a busy week."

"We had a busy week too," Elaine told her.

"Oh? A new mystery to solve?"

"Mostly tearoom stuff. We're preparing for an Autumn Tea event a week from Wednesday." She didn't feel that she should reveal that they were helping Dan investigate a real police matter, albeit from a strictly unofficial angle.

"Amy finds out whether the baby is a girl or boy that day," Jan told Sasha, "and we're going to have a gender reveal during the Autumn Tea if Amy agrees to it. You should try to come by."

Sasha's face lit with excitement. "Oh, I can't wait. I'll look at my calendar. Oops, gotta go!" She waved as Brody pulled her away. "We'll save you seats in 'your' pew."

"Hey." An urgent masculine voice behind the cousins made them turn simultaneously. Dan stood right behind them, Charlotte trailing him with their children, who were claiming her attention to show her projects they had made in Sunday school. "I saw you talking to Penny Jillette," he said. "Did you learn anything?"

"It sounds like they think they have pretty solid evidence," Elaine said. "But guess what? I'm going to be volunteering at HMH beginning Tuesday morning for a week or two."

"What?" Dan looked incredulous. "How did you manage that?"

"Quite easily, actually," Jan said, grinning. "We hope it will be helpful to have someone on the inside, as it were."

"It sure can't hurt," Dan said. "That's amazing. What's the solid evidence she mentioned?" His excitement seemed to drain out of him with the question.

Elaine related what Penny had said about the checks found in Alex's desk.

Dan's eyes narrowed in concentration. "Checks? You're sure it was checks and not cash?"

Both cousins nodded.

"That increases the odds that it's someone in the office then," Dan said. "Anybody could steal cash, but stealing checks, which you then have to convert to cash, is a whole new level. To steal checks, the thief had to literally be on site."

"Right, as opposed to having access to the accounts from a remote location," Jan said.

"Or to cash amounts being donated," Elaine said, "which could go missing in any number of ways."

"Bottom line," Dan said to Elaine, "you need to check out the other office workers. It almost *has* to be someone who has daily access to incoming checks."

CHAPTER FOUR

After church and lunch, Bob and Nathan, Elaine's boyfriend, came over. The two couples had planned an autumn hike on the trails at Lake St. George State Park, about ten miles to the east of Lancaster.

They were about to pile into Nathan's Cadillac when Jan said, "Oh! I forgot that open house across the street is today. Guys, would you mind if we just took a teeny little tour before we go to the lake?"

Bob chuckled. "A teeny little tour? Absolutely."

"I have to admit," Elaine said as she took Nathan's hand and started across the street, "I'd like to see it too. Victorian homes have such character."

The house had been well cared for, they knew. Mrs. Battie had a new roof put on just last year, and the landscaping was nicely trimmed, although there was little color now that autumn had set in. They mounted the wide front steps, admiring the shady front porch that led to a large veranda at the right side.

"I've always liked this color scheme," Jan said. The exterior of the house was painted a soft taupe shade with warm ivory paint on the porches, columns, and Italianate bracket trim, and with touches of dark chocolate accenting the decorative window frames and other embellishments. The three colors blended perfectly, projecting a warmth that could bring the house to life even in a dull winter landscape.

The front door was actually a set of wide wooden paneled doors with a half-moon window set in each and a large half moon transom window arching above both. As Jan reached for the knob, the door opened and a woman with short, stylish blonde hair said, "Jan and Elaine, how good to see you. In the market for another Victorian?"

"Hi, Sharon. We're probably more in the 'just nosy' category." Jan smiled warmly at the real estate agent. "I think we've both been looking for an excuse to see the place."

Sharon Reddick chuckled, extending her hand as Jan and Elaine introduced Bob and Nathan. She wore a smart gray pantsuit with accents of gold jewelry and low, dressy gray suede boots. "Please come in. I don't blame you at all for wanting to view this home. It's lovely." She handed Jan and Elaine each a spec sheet. "This house was built in 1840 in the Italianate design. The paint colors, both exterior and interior, are modern, so I can't tell you what the authentic historic colors would have been, but Mrs. Battie did a lovely job choosing complementing shades when she last repainted. As you'll see, this house is a little smaller than your home, only two stories with the little cupola up above that. There are three bedrooms and two and a half baths. There is also a full basement."

"Has it been extensively remodeled?" Jan asked.

Sharon shook her head. "Most of the interior wood trim is original. Of course, the biggest renovations needed would include the kitchen and both baths. They've been modernized, although they are not terribly up-to-date. But the roof was replaced last year, and the water heater is brand new. Both fireplaces have been converted to gas logs. Please feel free to look at your leisure. The formal parlor is to the right, and the family parlor is on the left."

"Thank you," Elaine said. "Oh, Jan, look at that staircase."

The four of them moved farther into the wide foyer, following the direction Elaine pointed. The balusters supporting the stair railing were clearly custom designed. "I believe that's cherry," Sharon said. "Isn't it gorgeous?"

"It is." Jan turned to her right, after noting the closet built into the space beneath the stairs.

Following Jan, the group entered a spacious room that continued the lovely crown molding around the tops of the walls and windows. It was empty, making it seem even bigger. A large marble fireplace took up the interior wall, while floor-to-ceiling windows with interior shutters graced the front and back walls. A set of french doors on the far side opened onto the veranda, from which a set of steps led down to a covered pass-through driveway. A detached garage stood behind the house.

Across the hall, the second parlor had been slightly modernized. "This must have been a dining room," Elaine said, noting a lower-hanging chandelier in the middle of the room. There was a smaller marble fireplace in the room, with a linen closet at one side, and a door leading into the kitchen at the other side.

Jan led the way into the kitchen. "This is what I really want to see," she said eagerly.

Once all four of them were in the kitchen, there was silence. Finally, Nathan said, "Shades of the '70s."

"This looks an awful lot like my mother's kitchen once did," Bob agreed, and the others all chuckled.

The appliances were a color called harvest gold that had been popular in the '70s, except for the black refrigerator, which clearly was a replacement. The stovetop had four coil burners, with pull-out drawers beneath, and the oven was wall-mounted next to it in the middle of more cabinets. The countertops sported white Formica with odd gold flower shapes that also probably had been all the rage forty years ago; the same Formica covered the breakfast island.

Still, the room was bright and cheerful, with a breakfast nook at the back of the room surrounded by a bay window.

"It has potential," Elaine announced. "Although since a kitchen renovation would be desirable, they may have to lower that asking price a little."

A door facing the right side led to the hallway, and they trooped in that direction.

In the hallway, they could see that it led back to the front foyer, or to a door with a storm screen at the back. Exiting through that door, they found themselves facing the back of the wrap-around porch with another set of steps leading to the garage just a few feet away. A branch of the path led to a square flagstone terrace with large stone planters marking each corner.

"Oh, that's lovely," Jan said. "What a pleasant spot for a meal in good weather."

"And look," Bob said. "Mrs. Battie must have kept a garden." Beyond the terrace there was a significantly sized plot of raw earth, now sporting a stellar crop of yellowing weeds, where stalks and stakes indicated there had indeed been a garden perhaps only a little more than a year ago.

Retracing their steps, the group reentered the house. Along the hallway right across from the kitchen were two small rooms. One was a pantry with built-in shelving around three sides, and the other was a laundry room and half bath. While the laundry and half bath could use updating, the washer and dryer were without question the newest appliances in the house.

Returning along the hallway to the staircase, the two couples then climbed to the second floor. There were only three bedrooms there, the fourth having been remodeled to be a master bedroom closet and a large master bath. A second bath was farther along the hall beside one of the remaining bedrooms. There was no interior access to the cupola, which was really nothing more than a decorative feature.

"It's definitely smaller than our house," Elaine said, "but it's quite charming."

The real estate agent had come to the top of the stairs in time to hear Elaine's comment. "I agree," she said. "I hope buyers feel that way. These larger, older homes are becoming increasingly more difficult to sell in a reasonable amount of time, particularly when they need updating like this one does."

"It doesn't need that much work," Jan protested. "The kitchen is the main thing."

"And the bathrooms," Bob said. "They could use a facelift too."

"But they're definitely livable," Jan said. "Anyone who can't see past the little details needed to update this lovely lady doesn't deserve her anyway." She turned to Elaine. "Too bad we're not younger and more ambitious. We could buy it and expand our business model."

"How so?" Elaine asked, bemused.

Jan was on a roll now. "We could put in a full-fledged restaurant over here, with private rooms upstairs for special events, and the terrace in the back—"

"Sadly, we're neither younger nor more ambitious," Elaine said, grinning as she rolled her eyes. "As busy as Tea for Two has grown, it's all I can do to keep up with that." Elaine signaled to Bob to move Jan along. "Come on, dreamer, let's go hiking."

Monday morning was busy. Rue Maxwell and Macy Atherton were the first two customers through the door in the morning, and they soon were followed by a plethora of others, locals as well as autumn tourists enjoying the crisp days that warmed up in the middle and were cool enough for crackling blazes in the fireplace at night.

Archie came in first thing to assist, and Rose arrived at noon to relieve the cousins, who were slated to meet Dan and his friend Alex at Dan's house at 1 p.m. Fortunately, business slacked off by 12:30, so the cousins were able to get away with fifteen minutes to spare. They had decided to walk, since Dan's home was less than six blocks away, and the autumn day was pleasantly warm and sunny beneath a cloudless blue sky.

As they stepped out the door of Tea for Two and walked along the drive to Main Street, Jan sighed, looking across the street at the Battie home. "I loved that house. Are we certain we don't want to open a restaurant?" She elbowed Elaine to show that she was joking as Elaine chuckled.

"I don't know about you, but I am dead certain," Elaine said. "I've enjoyed our tearoom adventure. But enlarging the business would take all the fun out of it, I fear."

"You're right," Jan said. "The bottom line is, I really just want to get my hands on that house and renovate the kitchen properly."

Elaine laughed out loud. "You'd like to renovate every kitchen you've ever been in 'properly,' I bet."

As the cousins turned off Main Street and began to walk along the sidewalk on Pine Ridge Road, Elaine said, "I'm anxious to meet this Alex today and hear what he has to say."

"I know," Jan said. "I hope Dan's faith in his friend is justified."

"Dan's generally an excellent judge of character," Elaine pointed out. "I suppose my worry is that such long acquaintance may have clouded his judgment in this instance."

"Anything's possible," Jan agreed. "Although Dan seems too levelheaded not to recognize that he could be cutting a dear friend too much slack. I'd be more inclined to think that Dan would bend over backward to ensure he *wasn't* being too lenient."

"Good point." After a moment, the cousins began to discuss their plans for the Autumn Tea, remaining on the subject until they turned into Dan's sidewalk a few minutes later.

The Benson home was a snug bungalow painted white, trimmed with a soft blue on the shutters and door that blended nicely with the gray shingled roof. A wide front porch ran along the entire front of the house, and a trio of dormer windows perched above the front door. An attached garage stood to the right of the house, and there was an unfamiliar black compact car parked in the driveway before it.

Elaine pivoted around a child's plastic Little Tikes push car, while Jan carefully stepped over a crudely drawn dinosaur image done in sidewalk chalk. Jan grinned. "Looks like someone's been enjoying the sunshine."

As they mounted the three shallow brick steps, passing an ornamental flower bed with a bird bath, Jan said, "This place has always been gorgeous from spring to fall." She pointed to the luxurious landscaping at either side of the steps and the side of the house. "And look! They've got witch hazel, saucer magnolia, forsythia, lilacs, and weigela here."

"I know," Elaine said. "There's that huge rhododendron over there by the garage, and I love how gorgeous that hedge of spirea is in the spring."

"That's one thing I'd do with the Battie house," Jan said. "Color would add a lot to the landscape plan."

Elaine laughed. "You're obsessed."

The interior door opened then, and Charlotte pushed open the storm door. "Good afternoon, ladies. Great to see you, although the occasion isn't so great." Her smile was warm, but her green eyes held worry. "Please come in. Alex is already here."

Charlotte took their jackets and hung them in a closet just inside the door before leading them through the hallway past a brown-and-cream living room that boasted a piano and a small brick fireplace, where a woman sat with a small baby in her arms while the Bensons' daughter played nearby.

Charlotte stopped. "This is Christa DeRone. Christa, Elaine Cook and Jan Blake, the ladies I was telling you about. And this is her son, Miles."

"It's nice to meet you," Christa said. "Thank you for helping us." Her eyes were suspiciously bright, and Elaine suspected she'd been crying.

"How old is Miles?" Jan asked. "He's darling."

"Six months," Christa said, "but three months adjusted. He was twelve weeks premature."

"Wow." Both cousins were startled.

"He was born at twenty-eight weeks?" Jan asked.

Christa nodded. "We had a few tense moments, but he's doing well now. Just a little small."

He certainly was, Elaine thought. Most children were sitting up and looking alert at six months. Miles was swaddled in a blanket in her arms like a much younger baby. Which, she supposed he was, just as Christa had said. "So, you called his age 'adjusted' because he's meeting milestones later than his age-mates?" Elaine asked.

Christa nodded. "It helps people not to have such big expectations."

"How long," Jan asked, "is it before children born prematurely catch up to their peers?"

"Answers differ depending on who you talk to," Christa told her. "But generally, between ages two and three, things even out. And, of course, the earlier the birth, the longer it may be until they catch up."

"I hope he continues to do well," Jan said sincerely.

Elaine nodded. "It was nice to meet you," she added.

Charlotte led them away then. In the dining room, the walls were a pale yellow and there were soft green accents in the fabric of the chair upholstery and a ceramic plate displayed on a sideboard. Dan and another man were seated at the table; both rose when the cousins entered. Alex was tall, probably two inches over Dan's six feet, with brown eyes and curly copper hair that fell over one side of his forehead.

Dan picked up the toddler who'd been sitting on his lap and handed her to his wife. "You'd better take this monkey for a while," he said to Charlotte, smiling.

"Hi, Winnie," Elaine said, waving to the little girl who had her mother's warm brown curls paired with Dan's blue eyes. "How are you today?" Both Jan and Elaine knew the Bensons' children from church.

Winnie grinned, showing perfect, pearly little teeth, and then very seriously spoke a string of words that were totally unintelligible to Elaine.

"That's wonderful," Elaine said, widening her eyes dramatically.

Dan chuckled as Charlotte whisked the tot away, and the cousins advanced into the room. "She's still pretty hard to understand. Do you know what she said?"

"Not a word," Elaine said, grinning, and all three of the others around the table laughed.

"Doesn't matter," Dan pronounced. "You faked it well." The mirth faded then. "This is Alex DeRone. Alex, Elaine Cook and Jan Blake, the ladies I told you about."

Alex DeRone shook each of their hands gravely. "Mrs. Cook. Mrs. Blake."

"Please," Elaine said, "call us Elaine and Jan."

"All right." Alex didn't seem to know what else to say, so Elaine took a seat as Jan did the same, and the men followed suit.

"As I told you," Dan began, speaking to Alex, "Elaine and Jan are pretty good at investigating and figuring out things that are not what they seem. Although we have never worked together officially, I can tell you they've solved several outright crimes and helped people unravel personal mysteries more than a few times in the two-plus years since they opened the tearoom."

"I appreciate your interest in my case," Alex said to the cousins. "But before we go any further, I need to ask your rates."

"Oh gracious, no, we couldn't accept money!" Jan exclaimed, just as Elaine said, "No rates. This is not a formal business."

Alex just stared at them. "But I can't ask you—"

"You didn't, and neither did Dan," Elaine said firmly. "We offered. So why don't you tell us what you can about your office, your arrest, and what you think could have happened?"

Alex drew a deep breath. "Thank you." He was silent a moment, marshalling his thoughts. "I'm not sure where to start," he admitted. "Dan said he told you I was arrested and charged with theft. They are talking about adding embezzlement charges too. The police say they found several checks hidden in my desk. But I swear to you that I never stole a single one of them."

"What's the first time you recall hearing about something being amiss?" Jan asked.

"Thursday morning," Alex said promptly. "Two troopers came into the building and asked to speak to me. I assumed they came to me because I was the CEO. I invited them back to my office, where they questioned me about missing checks. I was very cooperative. I had no idea they suspected me of wrongdoing and told them that they were free to examine our books, that there were no checks missing to my knowledge. They asked if they could search the room and I said yes. Why wouldn't I? I had nothing to hide. But then they found several envelopes containing donors' checks in the bottom drawer of my desk, hidden under some other things, and they eventually determined that those checks had never been entered in our donations account." He was visibly upset. "I have no idea how those checks got there."

CHAPTER FIVE

Alex dropped his head, staring at his hands clasped together on the table. His knuckles were white.

"Were the dates on the checks recent?" Jan asked.

Alex nodded. "They had to have come into the office within the last week. Maybe even the same day."

"Can you tell us who works in your office who could have had access to the checks?" Elaine thought it might be helpful to have an idea whom she'd be meeting tomorrow.

Alex sighed. "There are only four people in the office, other than me, and it would be really tricky to steal donations. I have no idea how it could be done. Our office manager, Ted Harrington, is a stickler for proper procedure. He logs in every mailed donation as it arrives. At least, that's how it works with checks," he said with a grim twist of his lips. "When we have fund-raisers that generate cash, Ted is the one who takes a locked cashbox to the office and then he counts it in the presence of another staff member—it isn't always the same person—before he enters it."

He fell silent, and Elaine cleared her throat. "And who are those other people?"

"There's a public relations coordinator, Penny Jillette, but she has very little to do with the actual donations. She works on publicity and promotion, donor outreach, that sort of thing. The CFO is Mitch Ackerly. He's as committed to HMH as the rest of us. And the only other person with an office is R.J. Dupree, our project coordinator. He oversees everything we have going on, communicates with the onsite project managers, orders materials, and things like that. He's out of the office a lot." Alex looked utterly miserable. "I like them all. We're a tight team. I honestly can't imagine any of them embezzling funds from HMH."

"How long have you worked there?" Elaine asked. She didn't comment on his last statement, since obviously he didn't know his coworkers as well as he thought he did.

"Three years," Alex said. "I love it." For a moment, his face lit up. "I have an older brother who was career army. He lost a leg in Afghanistan six years ago when he stepped on an IED, and ever since then, I've wanted to find a way to do something for wounded warriors. Homes for Maine's Heroes has been a dream for me." His face fell. "I can't believe this happened. It's like a nightmare, and I keep thinking I'll wake up. I just want things to go back to the way they were before those two cops walked into my office."

"Does anyone in your office need money badly that you know of?" Dan asked. "Or spend lavishly?"

"No one lives outside his or her means, I don't think. Mitch is independently wealthy, so his means are a little bigger than the others." He gave a wry chuckle. "Ted can be a little intense, but I can't imagine him embezzling from HMH. Penny and her husband don't have kids yet and they just bought their first home, but it was a modest purchase and should have been well within their means. And R.J.'s only a few years away from retirement. All he talks about are his grandkids." Alex shook his head in disbelief. "I can't believe that one of my coworkers would have set me up."

They spoke with Alex for a while longer, learning more about his history and that of the nonprofit, but they didn't learn anything particularly helpful. Walking back to the tearoom afterward, the cousins were silent at first.

Finally, Elaine heaved a sigh. "Time for a Google search, I think," she said.

"I agree," Jan said. "Is Alex DeRone really as squeaky-clean as he appears?"

"And if he's not," Elaine asked, "why would he take such a risk? If he embezzled that money, he's destroyed his career and his family for it."

"Not to mention," Jan said soberly, "his relationship with Dan, who absolutely believes he's innocent."

Elaine sighed. "I'm praying, for Dan's sake, that he is. But I'm keeping an open mind during this investigation."

When they arrived at Tea for Two after their afternoon walk home from Dan's home, Elaine and Jan went straight to the office by mutual accord.

"Want a cup of tea?" Jan asked.

Elaine grinned. "You read my mind."

"And maybe something sweet," Jan suggested. "I'll be back."

Elaine booted up her computer and typed in her password, then went online to a search engine and typed in Alex's name. A list of hits immediately came up.

Jan returned with a tray bearing a large pot and two cups of tea, as well as two crème de menthe brownies with their narrow layer of mint green sandwiched between two layers of dark, luscious chocolate.

"I wonder," Elaine said, "how much weight I've gained since we opened this business."

"None," Jan said. "We work off the calories most of the time. My weight gain was a fluke." She referred to a handful of pounds she had gained and then worked hard to lose a few months ago. But she winked as she handed Elaine a plate.

"If you say so," Elaine chuckled, taking the fork and dessert Jan handed to her. "There are a whole lot of mentions of Alex DeRone online," she said. "This could take a while. He's been working at HMH for three years, and you can bet they've done a ton of publicity during that time."

"Can you arrange them by date?" Jan asked.

"Not exactly," Elaine said. "But I could probably search by year and read through one year at a time to get a sense of the time line."

"Oh, that's a good plan. I could take a year to look through tonight if you like. Right now, I have to work on a couple of recipes for tomorrow while Rose and Archie are still here to handle the customers."

While Jan worked in the kitchen with their employees, Elaine used the remainder of the afternoon to read through articles about Alex DeRone.

Many of them were publicity pieces, released to the press online with the goal of raising the nonprofit's profile in the community. Some were local, but some were statewide. Alex traveled around the state speaking about HMH's mission, and those appearances were chronicled as well. Fund-raising, of course, was the end goal of those press pieces and appearances. The more people who knew about HMH, and the higher the company's profile in regard to the good work they were doing, the more money they could persuade people to donate.

How much money was the company pulling in now? Elaine couldn't help but wonder, given Penny's comment about over half a million dollars having been embezzled. Quickly, she opened a new search and went to the company's website. As she'd hoped, there were financial statements for the previous three fiscal years. It was easy to see the influence Alex had been having. In the past three years, income had grown from just over three million to seven and a half. It seemed like an enormous amount of money for a small organization in a small community, but she reminded herself that HMH served the whole state of Maine, despite its physical location in Waterville.

Returning to the search on Alex, she began to read. There were interviews in which Alex and the board president spoke of the company's goals. There were partnerships with local and state groups who raised funds for a particular veteran's home or for the charity at large. There was an annual thirty-six-hour online fund-raising event in which the amount they raised was matched by a percentage from a local charitable support organization. They had done well in that event, Elaine noted, nabbing the second place overall and earning an extra thousand-dollar prize.

Finally, she began to find earlier information. There was an article summarizing Alex's first year with Homes for Maine's Heroes in which he spoke of how much he had learned and enumerated his goals for the future. Goals, she noted, that appeared to be well on their way toward being met now, three years into that future.

Next, she saw that he had joined the Waterville Area Chamber of Commerce, the Mid-Maine Chamber of Commerce that served a larger area, and even the Maine State Chamber of Commerce. All were clever moves, she thought. Since his organization served all of Maine, he was looking for ways to widen the pool of potential donors.

It was exactly what she would have done in his position.

Then she came upon several news accounts from various papers about Alex's hiring in the wake of the last CEO's departure. Apparently, the former CEO had done little to grow the organization and had even gotten into an ugly public spat with the Waterville mayor. He'd been asked to resign; unwritten was the second half of that sentence: *or he'd be fired.*

The charity had limped along for several months with no leader as the board managed it and conducted a search for a new CEO. Alex and two others had been the top contenders, but Alex had come away with the job offer. Elaine made a note of his salary. It seemed well within a normal range for a three-million-dollar nonprofit, which it had been when he'd started.

Over and over again, members of the search committee voiced their confidence in Alex. Their pleasure in finding someone who appeared to be a team player was obvious, and having the advantage of seeing Alex's success in the position, she imagined those search committee members were feeling pretty good about their decision—until now.

The read-through was going faster than she'd anticipated. Many of the search engine's hits linked to the same articles, so there actually wasn't as much material as she and Jan had anticipated at first. As she clicked and brought up a new page of older search results, she was pleased to see that she finally had found some things that predated Alex's hiring.

There was his departure from a bank where he had worked as a commercial lender after he graduated from the University of Southern Maine with a BS in Business Administration and Marketing. The bank president heaped accolades on him and said they were sorry to see him go. He joked that he hoped Alex would think of his old friends for HMH's lending needs in the future.

In an article unrelated to his career, Alex was mentioned in his grandfather's obituary. He also was mentioned as the committee chair of a Santa's Gifts drive through the bank for underprivileged children, and he participated in several volunteer positions with the chambers of commerce to which he now belonged. Additional articles featured his brother, Kent, the one Alex had told them about. The articles had popped up in her search because Alex was quoted in them numerous times, apparently the family spokesman while his elder brother was incapacitated.

The articles detailed the loss of Kent's leg to an IED, a fellow soldier's heroic lifesaving effort to keep him alive until he could be evacuated to a triage area, his initial surgery and recuperation in Germany and later at a rehab center in the States, and finally, a hero's welcome home to Maine, where he was a recipient of one of the first homes built by the newly formed Homes for Maine's Heroes nonprofit.

Elaine was just about ready to stop searching, feeling she'd gone back far enough, when she came across a letter to the editor Alex had written during his commercial banking tenure. It predated his brother's injury by several years.

> *When I first learned about the formation of Homes for Maine's Heroes, I was enthusiastic. I was prepared to offer my full support to this worthy organization that supports our wounded warriors. Unfortunately, I can no longer say I am enthusiastic or supportive of HMH, after learning that the current CEO's salary is well over $100,000. That's right, folks. WELL over $100,000.*
>
> *Do I believe the job is critical? Absolutely I do. The CEO of any nonprofit needs to wear many hats. He or she must be personable, well organized, energetic, and capable of analyzing reports and making informed decisions. He or she must interact with the public in a positive way that reflects well on the organization in order to bring in the funds necessary for such an expensive endeavor as*

building multiple homes with special-needs features. And he or she must have numerous other skills critical to helping a nonprofit succeed.

Is that job worth $100,000 in compensation? After conducting a survey of other nonprofits in the area, I found that a huge salary such as this is completely out of line. Understanding that many nonprofits are far smaller and do not have an operating budget the size of HMH's, I extracted a smaller comparative list of only those nonprofits whose operating budgets are similar in size. Not a single one of their CEOs makes over $80,000, and only one CEO earns that benchmark salary, one man who has been with his organization for over twenty-five years.

I am deeply disappointed to see that HMH compensates its CEO with such a lavish, over-the-top salary while veterans struggling with disabilities often do not even receive a living wage. Men and women who gave their lives and parts of their bodies in service to our nation deserve better, and I find it sad and ironic that an organization devoted to helping deserving veterans would pay anyone so well. It is with deepest regret that I find I can no longer support HMH with my donations or my fund-raising efforts.

Elaine sat back in her chair. "Whoa."

"What?" Jan entered the room at the exact moment the words left Elaine's lips. "Did you find something important?"

"I don't know," Elaine said slowly. She beckoned to Jan, rolling her chair aside so Jan could see the monitor and read the letter to the editor.

"Whoa is right," Jan said in a heartfelt tone as she finished reading. "I take it Alex was not employed at HMH when he wrote this."

Elaine shook her head. Quickly, she gave Jan a chronological encapsulation of all she had learned. She consulted the little notepad on which she'd been jotting things down. "Alex draws a salary of $65,000 now," she told Jan. "He started at just under $60,000, and has received raises each year."

"And you know this...how?"

"HMH shares their previous three years' estimated and actual expenses on their website as well as the results of the IRS audit. They also shared this year's budget after it was approved by the board. Then I consulted a 'charity watchdog' website that ranks charities based on their transparency, their effectiveness, and how much of their donated income goes to operating expenses—which consist of administration and fund-raising—and how much goes to program services, those that directly support the charity's mission."

"So, you learned how much he's made. What did you learn about how he's handling the organization?"

Elaine gave her a thumbs-up. "He's a terrific CEO as far as I can see. HMH receives an *A* from this website, which means they pour at least seventy-five percent of their money back into their charitable efforts, and their fund-raising and admin costs are kept pretty low."

Jan looked at the figures Elaine had jotted on her pad. "When he was hired, his salary was just over half of what they had paid the previous guy. And even though it's risen, it's still nowhere near what that guy was making when he was asked to leave."

"Correct."

"I wonder," Jan said thoughtfully, "if he has trouble living on his salary."

"I don't know," Elaine said, "but I think we need to keep in mind the possibility that Alex DeRone could be our guilty party."

CHAPTER SIX

Elaine kept her own words about Alex's possible guilt in mind as she dressed and ate breakfast the following morning. Her morning devotional had, by interesting chance, discussed new beginnings, using several Scriptures. Perhaps, she thought, it wasn't simply chance. Going to the HMH offices as an "undercover investigator" was certainly a sort of new development in the amateur mystery-solving that she and Jan so enjoyed.

"Wish me luck," she said to Jan as she buttoned the green-and-brown tweed wool jacket she had paired with a short-sleeved cream sweater and a knee-length skirt in leaf brown that brought out the same shades in the jacket. Low-heeled brown pumps with stylish blocky heels and a green scarf completed her ensemble along with simple gold jewelry. She had neglected to ask Penny what the dress code at HMH was, and she hoped business casual was a safe choice.

"Or should I say 'happy hunting'?" Jan teased.

Elaine grinned before picking up the lunch she'd packed and slinging her handbag over her shoulder. "Given the goal, that sounds appropriate."

"Either way, I'll certainly pray for you," Jan said.

Elaine drove the ten miles to Waterville and followed her directions to the HMH offices, which were housed on the second floor of a two-story traditional brick building fronted by an overhang with white columns. The charity was near the back of an office complex with four similar buildings arranged around a central parking lot. As she parked, she noted that doctors and dentists, hair salons, insurance offices, a veterinarian, a travel agency, and other small businesses were discreetly identified on tasteful signs at each front door.

She walked up the sidewalk and opened the heavy entry door, then stepped into a small foyer. The right half of the first floor was occupied by a broker's office. The other side appeared to be unoccupied at present.

The steps to HMH were directly ahead, with a discreet elevator next to them. A small accent table stood at one side, and a coat tree at the other, although both currently were empty.

Glancing to her right, she saw, through the glass door of the office, a woman seated behind a desk, who smiled and waved before turning her attention back to her work. A friendly face was a good omen, Elaine decided, taking a deep breath and mounting the steps, which rose to a small landing and switched back to rise the rest of the way to the second floor.

The layout upstairs was somewhat different, designed for one larger business rather than two small offices like the main floor, with a glass entry door straight ahead at the top of the second landing. Pulling open the door, Elaine found herself looking at a small, tastefully furnished foyer with a reception window and a door to her left just past the elevator entrance.

A young-looking man seated at a desk in the office behind the window rose to his feet and came to slide open the glass. He wore charcoal-gray wool trousers, a crisp white button-down shirt and burgundy tie with a pink-and-gray paisley pattern. A matching suit jacket was neatly hung over the back of his office chair. "Good morning and welcome to Homes for Maine's Heroes. How can I help you?"

The man was about her size. Despite his youthful looks, he had thinning blond hair combed over from a side part. He radiated professionalism, if not exactly warmth.

"Good morning," Elaine said. "I'm here to meet with Penny Jillette about volunteering."

"Oh, you must be Elaine. She told me to expect you. She ran to the post office, but she'll be back momentarily." The window promptly slid shut. A moment later, the door opened. "Please come in. I'm Ted Harrington, the office manager." He extended his hand and gave hers a brisk shake when she accepted, then dropped it and turned. "Follow me. I'll introduce you and give you a quick tour."

Elaine followed Ted down a hallway as he pointed out rooms they were passing. "Conference room. Restrooms. Kitchen. I presume that's your lunch?" He pointed at the insulated bag she carried.

Elaine nodded.

"You can stash that in the fridge," Ted told her. "The only rule is that leftovers all have to be taken home on Friday. None of us has the time or inclination to clean out dozens of containers with penicillin experiments growing in them."

Turning the Tables

Elaine smiled, but stifled it quickly when she saw that the office manager wasn't trying to be funny.

"Also, the coffeemaker is for general use. Again, the rule is that if you make it, you clean it out when it's empty or at the end of the day. Right now, Penny and I usually take turns since we're the ones most likely to make and drink it. Also, no dishes in the sink."

The rooms he had just pointed out were all on the left. Then he stopped between two doorways a little farther on. "This is Penny's office." He indicated the one on the left. Then he turned to the right. "And over here is our project coordinator's office. This is R.J. Dupree. He oversees all the building tasks we have going on at any one time. All the project managers report to him."

A burly man with thick white hair looked up from a set of blueprints, his hazel eyes twinkling. "Welcome to HMH. Who do I have the pleasure of addressing?" He smiled warmly. He wore a sky-blue sport shirt with the HMH logo on the breast and khaki pants, a more casual look than Ted had chosen.

"Elaine Cook," she said, stepping forward to shake his outstretched hand. "I'm going to be helping Penny with a volunteer project."

"And she's doing cartwheels about it," he assured her. "She told me this morning not to make too many bad puns and scare you away."

Elaine laughed. "It would take more than that to scare me away."

"Good, good. Hey, you run the tea place in Lancaster, right?"

61

"Yes." Elaine assumed Penny had mentioned that as well.

"I think you're going to meet my wife next week. She's signed up to go help with some charity quilting thing there."

"Oh yes! That's our event. I'll look forward to meeting her." Ted, she noticed, was already moving off, and she waved a hasty goodbye to R.J. before following Ted farther down the hallway.

"You probably won't see a lot of R.J.," Ted told her. "He travels to the various building sites a good bit, wrangles supplies, and generally oversees all the actual building. He's usually out of here by ten."

He stopped in between another pair of offices, then turned to face the open door on his left.

"Mitch, this is Elaine Cook. She's going to be helping Penny with a volunteer project. Elaine, Mitch Ackerly, our chief financial officer."

A pleasant-looking man of average height came around his desk to shake her hand. His eyes and hair were both coffee brown, his handshake firm. She noticed his necktie had been loosened and his sleeves rolled halfway up his forearms, unlike Ted's crisp business look or R.J.'s more casual one. "Welcome to HMH. Thanks for volunteering your time."

"You're welcome," Elaine said. "I admire the work all of you do. HMH is a great asset to our area and to the entire state."

"We think so too," Mitch said, eyes twinkling. "We're a pretty dedicated team here."

"Across the hallway is the CEO's office," Ted said, moving on as Mitch returned to his desk. "But he is not in this week."

Did the man really think she wasn't aware of what had occurred? Elaine opened her mouth and then closed it again as he opened the door at the end of the hall.

"And this," he said, "is our supply/storage/cleaning products room. I can't imagine you'll need to be in here though."

Elaine felt like a student with a particularly stern principal reviewing the rules. *Don't leave leftovers in the fridge. Clean up your dishes. Don't go into the storage room.*

"Ah," said Ted, a distinct note of relief in his tone. "Here's Penny. She's all yours!" he called to Elaine's friend at the far end of the hallway. Then he simply turned and walked all the way back to his office without another word.

Elaine blinked. Then she shrugged off the man's offhand behavior and walked toward Penny's office.

Penny wore black leggings with black flats under a black-and-pink-checked dress. Her bright-red hair was bundled carelessly in a bun from which charming tendrils escaped and curled about her face and neck. Somehow, the color of her hair and the dress worked rather than clashing as Elaine would have expected. "Hi," Penny said, beckoning her in and indicating a chair near her desk. "Thank you so much for coming in. Did Ted show you around?"

Elaine nodded. "And he introduced me to Mitch and R.J." She held up her handbag. "The only thing he didn't tell me was where I might keep this."

"Oh, just hang it on the back of my door," Penny said. "Coat, purse, umbrella, whatever." She closed the door and placed her own jacket and handbag on the hooks revealed.

Elaine followed suit before taking her seat. "And my lunch is in the refrigerator."

"Great. I brought mine too. Maybe we can sit outside and eat later. There's a nice picnic table that R.J. built and set behind the building. I try to eat there when I can, although before long it'll be too cold. Sometimes Sally from downstairs eats there too. I'll introduce you."

Elaine nodded. "Lunch and a new friend. Sounds great. Tell me what we're going to be doing today."

Penny set aside a stack of folders on her desk and folded her hands. "HMH's tenth anniversary celebration is coming up. The organization incorporated ten years ago this coming January and completed its first home in July of the same year. Part of my job includes planning and carrying out a variety of celebratory activities designed, of course, to bring us to people's attention. While the mission of any nonprofit should be its central goal, another significant portion of the organization's responsibilities is to stay in the public eye, and as an outgrowth of that, attracting more donations to allow us to grow our mission."

"Do you believe there's a need for increased services?" Elaine didn't have any idea how many Maine veterans might need special accommodations in their homes, nor how many others, like injured firefighters or police, might need assistance.

"Oh yes." Penny nodded. "We currently have more requests for special housing than we can accommodate, and on top of that, we also have requests from others for alterations to existing homes to help wounded warriors manage their daily lives better. Alex, our CEO, has—" She stopped and swallowed. "*Had* a five-year-plan approved by the board to expand our organization to meet more of those needs. He hoped to use the anniversary as a springboard to increase publicity and bring in more donations."

"Alex is the man who was arrested last week." Elaine made it a statement rather than a question. Penny had told her that much already, and she wanted to steer the conversation in that direction.

Penny nodded, her expression troubled. "As I said, it's been terribly upsetting."

"I imagine so," Elaine said. "Did you have any idea?"

Penny shook her head, her freckled face distressed. "He's the nicest guy on the planet and an excellent boss. Organized, great ideas, good at making us feel valued while still giving us direction for improvement... I can't believe he stole money from the company."

"Is it possible there was a mistake?" Elaine was curious to see what the other HMH employees thought.

Penny shook her head again. "No, the police seemed pretty certain. And those checks were found in his desk and car, like I told you Sunday."

"In his car?" Elaine shook her head. "I hadn't heard that part."

"Oh yes." Penny nodded solemnly. "After they found the ones in his office, they searched his car. His house too, I think, although if they found anything there, I haven't heard about that."

Elaine was stunned. Alex hadn't mentioned any checks in his car when they'd spoken. Why not?

"I wonder why someone would embezzle money," she said thoughtfully, hoping to get Penny's take on that angle and hide her own disquiet about the newest revelation.

The younger woman shrugged. "I keep thinking about that. He doesn't live beyond his means that I know of. The only thing that came to mind is that his son was born about three months early and was in the hospital for weeks and weeks. We have decent insurance, but I imagine they had some deductible and out-of-pocket costs, and I wonder how much they actually ended up being responsible for."

Elaine recalled Alex's scathing letter regarding the former CEO's salary and his own, much lower one. Would medical bills be enough to make a man betray his principles? "Do you think the police knew where to look before they arrived? How were they alerted? Did someone here uncover missing money?"

"Ted told me one of our regular donors, Jean Briggs, got suspicious when she didn't get a thank-you for her tax files. Turns out she's Mitch's wife's aunt. Can you say 'awkward'? I believe she called in and talked to Ted, who referred her to Mitch, and poor Mitch is the one who had to ask Alex about it. When Alex didn't have a good explanation, the police got involved."

"It sounds very upsetting," Elaine said. "So, tell me what this project is and how I can help." The last thing she wanted was to appear too curious and alert Penny to her investigation of the theft. For all she knew, Penny could be involved, she realized suddenly. True, she thought it unlikely from what she knew of the young woman, but then again, Penny didn't seem to think Alex DeRone had been suspicious either.

Unaware of Elaine's thoughts, Penny said, "So here's the situation: HMH has dozens of photos from homes we've built and other projects we've done through the past decade. I'd like to do two things. First, I want to organize everything chronologically and pull together some of the best for a set of photo books that we can place in the lobby and take when we go out to do presentations. I'd also like to put together two PowerPoint presentations. One would be a general overview of a house from start to finish, including how we selected the family and their reaction to the final product. The second would be a montage of families in their new homes accompanied by one photo of some phase of construction on that house."

Elaine's eyebrows rose. "That's an ambitious project, but I think both the display books and the PowerPoints are a great idea."

"The PowerPoints would be fantastic visual backgrounds anytime we have an event," Penny agreed.

"Are the photos digital and therefore dated? Because then we could just order the files by date."

"Most are," Penny said, "but not all. We'll need to make sure we have dates on the ones that are not digital, and then see if there are any we want to use and scan them in."

Elaine grinned. "Another layer."

"I know." Penny looked a little frantic. "The idea is noteworthy, but when I realized how much time it was really going to take, I got a little panicked."

That made Elaine laugh. "Which is why you recruited me. Don't worry. I think it's a doable project in one to two weeks, and fortunately, I should be able to give you a good bit of time.

The only conflict I know I have is a week from tomorrow when we host our Autumn Tea at Tea for Two."

"That would be awesome." Penny looked thrilled. "Let's go down to the conference room. I set up a laptop and several boxes of photos there earlier this morning, so we can get right to work."

After following Penny to the conference room, Elaine sorted one of the boxes of photos. First, she laid out ten index cards with each of the past decade's years individually listed. Then she methodically began to go through the printed photos, trying to place them in a stack beneath the appropriate year's label.

While she did so, Penny took on the thousands of photos on the laptop, importing them into a program that would put them in order by the date taken rather than by the last date modified, which is what the default program was set up to do.

The work was fascinating at first. Many of the photos were dated on the back, making them easy to place chronologically, and some even had accounts of the subject and activity in the photo. *Rod Waring installs pull-down shelving in kitchen of Pfc. Benny Sneed's home while Phil Harmon measures the height needed to ensure countertops and appliances are wheelchair accessible,* read one such caption.

She quickly saw that wide doorways and hallways were necessary in homes for wheelchair-bound clients, as well as hardwood floors to make it easier to get around. Another major feature needed were accessible bathrooms, allowing veterans to transfer from wheelchair to toilet, and to roll right into a shower, where they could transfer to a seat. In existing homes, the same modifications could be made, as well as in some places lowering wall plates where light switches were difficult to reach, and building ramps over existing steps to ensure easy home entry for wheelchairs.

"No wonder you love working here," she said after picking up a photo of a smiling veteran with his wife by his wheelchair and their toddler on his lap.

Penny looked up from the computer and smiled. "It's pretty rewarding," she said. "I always wanted to work in the nonprofit sector, but this has met and exceeded all my expectations." She flicked a glance at the table, which was beginning to show some signs of organization. "How's it coming?"

"Pretty well. Most of them at least have a date on them. Those that don't, I placed in a box for us to go through. I guess the only way to date those will be to match them up with other digital photos taken of the same place or people."

"I can bring in another laptop so we both can work on that," Penny said.

Just then, Mitch stuck his head in. "How's it going in here?"

"Great," Penny said. "You headed out?"

Mitch nodded. "I've got meetings all day with a lunch sandwiched in between. Doing two jobs is keeping me hopping."

"You're meeting with donors?"

"Yep. I'm handling a couple of meetings Alex had scheduled before he left."

"I hope they go well," Penny said. "Let me know if you need any support from my end."

"All right then. See you in a bit," Mitch said, pushing off the doorway and disappearing.

Penny rolled her eyes. When she realized Elaine had seen her do it, she looked sheepish. "I was hired to handle PR and work with potential donors. Mitch seems to have forgotten that I could help with a lot of those meetings if he'd only ask."

"I thought he was your financial officer," Elaine said, hoping to learn more about him.

"He is. But I think he's hoping he'll get the CEO's job if Alex doesn't come back. He was our external auditor first, but when the accountant position came open, he really wanted it. Some family friend sits on the board and recommended him for the in-house position." She raised her eyebrows. "I know at least one board member was strongly opposed to his hiring at the time because of the dual role."

"Wait," Elaine said. "He's still your auditor as well as your accountant?"

"Not anymore," Penny said, "but there was an overlap of several months. I guess it's water under the bridge now, since they found a new auditor. And Mitch really has brought in quite a few high-dollar donors, mostly due to his wife's connections. So I get why Alex recommended to the board that they hire Mitch. Ultimately it was the right call."

Once again, Alex had proven to be a smart CEO. Would he really jeopardize that good reputation?

CHAPTER SEVEN

Elaine thought about what Penny had said about Mitch. "What type of connections does Mitch have?"

"Have you heard of Bettina Dacourt-Vallerand? She's his wife. And yes, she uses her whole name. She never goes by Ackerly. Her mother's and father's people both are very well-known, wealthy 'old Maine' families."

Elaine had heard the names Dacourt and Vallerand in connection with a number of philanthropic efforts around the state. "So he really is valuable in PR."

Penny sighed. "I know. But I would have loved to have more of a chance. Anyway, it's noon. Let's break for lunch."

The pair retrieved their lunches from the refrigerator. Checking the temperature, they saw that the high was a sunny sixty-two degrees, so they left their jackets. Penny led Elaine to the end of the hallway, where she opened the storage room door. They walked through the small space, lined on both sides with shelves and filing cabinets, and walked to an exit at the rear of the small room that Ted had not shown Elaine.

The door opened onto a set of sturdy metal stairs, and once at ground level, Elaine saw at the back of the building a lovely white birch tree whose leaves had mostly changed from green to golden. There was a flower bed at its base, currently sporting a handsome variety of chrysanthemums, beside which stood an octagonal cedar picnic table with attached seating.

A woman already sat there, reading a magazine, but she looked up with a smile as the pair approached.

"Hi, Sally," Penny said. "This is Elaine Cook. We attend church together, and she's my personal hero for the next week or two because she's helping me with that giant photo project I mentioned to you. Elaine, this is Sally Murray, the office manager at Edward Jones downstairs."

Sally, the woman who had smiled and waved at Elaine when she'd arrived, looked to be in her late thirties or early forties. She had heavily lashed dark-gray eyes that crinkled at the corners when she smiled and a sleek, straight bob of shiny ebony hair. "Hi, Elaine. Welcome to our lovely little luncheon area."

"Thank you."

"Better enjoy it," Sally said. "Any day now it's going to be too cold to eat out here."

"The almanac says first snow on November tenth," Penny commented.

"Noooo," Sally moaned. "I'm not ready for winter again."

"That's what my neighbor said," Elaine told her. "After her husband died, she put her house on the market and moved to Florida."

"Florida might be a little too hot and humid for me," Sally said. "What about the southern Mediterranean coast of Italy, where there are sea breezes to help cool you down?"

All three women sighed together.

Then Elaine laughed. "I lived in Italy for two years when my husband was stationed there. It's a lovely country."

"It is," Sally said. "I—"

"Hey, Sally," Penny interrupted, "would you consider helping Elaine and me if you can get away for a few hours some afternoon?"

Elaine looked at Penny in surprise, then quickly masked her expression. In her experience, Penny was not a rude person normally.

Sally appeared to take it in stride. "If Dennis closes the office on Thursday again, I probably could."

"Oh, that would be great," Penny said warmly. "Thanks."

"What's the latest on Alex?" Sally asked. "Is he in jail?"

"Of course not," Penny said, sounding indignant. "He's at home. I guess out on bail, but it's not like he's a flight risk."

"You never know," Sally said. "Which reminds me, how did they know those checks were stolen?"

Penny looked glum. "I think that when they found them, they went to Mitch and asked for our donor list. Apparently, the 'found' checks in the desk were from people who pledged regular monthly donations. They believe Alex knew these checks would be coming in and was on the lookout for them."

Elaine took another bite of her sandwich to prevent herself from entering the conversation. She desperately wanted to quiz the women even more, but they unwittingly were doing a pretty good job of giving her information.

The conversation made it clear that the starting point for the thefts—and potentially embezzlement—must be the mail. Who opened it and recorded the donations? Logic said either Ted, Mitch, or Alex.

"Ted's the one who brings in the mail and records everything, supposedly. So how did those checks get past him?" Penny shook her head. "I still can't believe Alex would do this."

Sally turned to Elaine. "You've met Ted, right?"

Elaine nodded. "Just this morning."

"Isn't he a hoot? They don't come much more rigid than our friend Ted."

Privately, Elaine agreed with that assessment, but she didn't want to encourage unkindness. "He took time out of his schedule to give me a mini-tour."

"Just don't mess with his mail routine," Penny advised with a grin.

"Mail routine?"

Penny nodded. "Ted has a system for dealing with the mail, and woe betide the person who interferes with it. I have certainly never been accorded the privilege of touching the sacred mail."

Which might mean it was less likely that Penny would have much opportunity to steal the checks. It might not clear her completely, but Elaine felt relief just the same. "What's his system?" she asked, responding to Penny's comment.

"You'll see," Penny said. "At eleven o'clock tomorrow, make some excuse to go into the front office, and you can witness it for yourself."

"It's memorable," Sally said. "I've seen it, and I can attest."

"Oh, look." Penny pointed to a car at the light at the corner, just visible from where they sat. "That's a Honda HR-V. That's what Derek and I are saving for." She sighed. "We're almost there, but not quite."

Sally rolled her eyes. "You know, you can borrow. A car loan is an asset on a credit report as long as your payment history is good."

"I know," Penny said, "but my credit rating is already great. I only keep two credit cards and I use them carefully. I really don't want more debt. Besides, if I pay for it outright, I'm actually paying a lot less than I would if I financed it."

Sally grinned. "I can't argue with that logic." She began to gather up her lunch things. "I've got to get back to work. Elaine, it was lovely to meet you. I'm sure I'll see you again."

"You as well," Elaine said, waving as Sally finished picking up and walked around the side of the building to a door near the base of the stairs Elaine and Penny had come down earlier.

The moment Sally was out of sight, Penny said, "I bet you think I'm the rudest person on the planet."

"How so?" Elaine suspected she was referring to the way she'd interrupted Sally earlier, but she could hardly agree.

"When Sally mentioned Italy, I jumped right in and cut her off. I adore Sally, but, well, how can I say this? She's a little bit obsessed with Italy. She will talk your ear off about all things

Italian given any opportunity. So consider this a friendly warning: don't give her the opportunity." She chuckled, and Elaine had to smile.

"Thanks for the heads-up."

AFTER DINNER THAT evening, Elaine sat down in her chair in the sitting room and opened her laptop. "I want to Google how to embezzle," she said to Jan. "I'm clearly not cut out to be a career criminal—I have no idea what anyone would do with those checks. Wouldn't they be hard to cash?"

"Funny you should mention that," Jan said. "I don't know enough about it to offer an opinion. Let's check it out."

After fifteen minutes spent fruitlessly chasing from one link to another that yielded little information, Elaine finally said, "Aha!" and looked up from her laptop, which she balanced across her legs in their sitting room.

"Aha?" Jan inquired.

"It looks as if an embezzler who steals checks must open a false account, forge the company's endorsement on a legitimate check, and then deposit the check into the fake account."

Jan thought about that for a moment. "Makes sense. So how do we find out if a bank holds an account that isn't a legit HMH one? Ask?"

Elaine snorted. "I kind of doubt a bank is going to give us information about any accounts other than our own. Discretion is one of the hallmarks of a good bank."

Jan nodded wryly, tapping her temple. "You're right. I'll have to think about this." She looked at her cousin. "Tell me everything you learned today."

Elaine detailed her day for Jan.

"A Honda HR-V doesn't cost half a million dollars," Jan pointed out. "And if Penny has little access to the mail, I still think she's probably in the clear."

"I agree, but we can't eliminate her completely," Elaine cautioned.

"And Alex is still in the mix." Jan looked disappointed. "I'd love to be able to tell Dan, 'Alex couldn't have done it, and here's why.'"

"Me too, but we're certainly not there yet," Elaine said. "As far as I know at this point, the people with access to the mail include the office manager, Ted; maybe the project coordinator, R.J.; maybe the CFO, Mitch Ackerly; maybe Penny if she was lying for some reason; and Alex himself."

"There could be others," Jan pointed out. "Board members."

"Could be," Elaine admitted. "That's something for me to find out in the coming days."

Jan chuckled. "I can't wait to hear about Ted's mail routine." Then she sobered as the import of the statement sank in. "So, I guess Ted Harrington goes straight to the top of our list of suspects."

"He's certainly right up there," Elaine agreed.

"Something occurs to me," Jan said. "How did the police know to check Alex's desk and car?"

Elaine's eyebrows rose. "*Hmm.* I hadn't thought about that. I don't know."

"Could someone have tipped them off? And if so, how do we find out who it was, because that person would look very suspicious to me."

"True, if indeed someone did give them a tip. But I think it's more likely that the investigators didn't know in advance to check Alex's desk. An employee's desk would be among the first places anyone would look for incriminating evidence. Maybe they just intended to start with Alex's and move on to the rest of the employees. But when they 'struck gold' on their first try, so to speak, they then searched his car."

Jan made a face. "You're probably right. So much for my brilliant detecting."

"We need to talk to him again anyway." Elaine told her.

"Why?"

"To ask him about the check found in his car," Elaine said.

Jan shook her head. "It looks bad that he didn't tell us about that."

"I know." Elaine's shoulders slumped.

Both cousins were silent for a moment, considering the implications.

Finally, Jan said, "It seems significant that the checks found in the desk were from recurring donors. Theoretically, anyone pocketing those donors' envelopes would know how much was inside them."

Elaine nodded. "And probably would know when they were coming in—like around the fifteenth of the month, for instance."

Jan pursed her mouth, thinking, and then jumped as her cell phone rang.

"It's Amy," Jan said as she checked the readout. "Hi, honey," she said to her daughter. "You're on speaker."

"Hi, Mom. Hi, Elaine."

"Hi, gorgeous," Elaine said. "How are you feeling?"

"Good," Amy said. "Really good now. I'm still having zero brilliant ideas about a gender reveal though, and I'm hoping you and Mom have come up with something."

"Actually," Jan said, "Elaine and I have been thinking... since the ultrasound is the day of our Autumn Tea, perhaps we could combine the two."

There was a momentary silence. "How?" Amy sounded doubtful.

"What if we had you come by the tearoom after your ultrasound?" Jan suggested. "We could put up a display next week and encourage all of our patrons to guess the gender. I was thinking of a big pumpkin and a sign that says, 'He or She: what will our little seed be?'"

"Oh, that's cute!" Amy exclaimed. "I like that."

"Good," her mother said. "Our customers would write their name on a guess and place it in a 'boy' or 'girl' basket, or something like that."

"And after we arrive, we can reveal the gender," Amy enthused.

"You can bet Rue and Macy and pretty much everyone who's excited about this baby will try to be there, and it's also the day we're having the quilting bee for the charity quilt, so there's sure to be a big group."

"This sounds like fun." Amy seemed really happy with the idea.

"And then," Jan added, "after you reveal the gender, a winner of a little gift of some kind will be pulled from the pool of correct guesses."

"We could wrap a selection of pastries," Elaine suggested, "or put together a few selections of autumn-themed teas."

"Oh, you two are brilliant," Amy said. "Thank you so much. I can't wait to tell my friends. I bet a lot of them will want to come by and make guesses too."

Jan and Amy chatted a while longer. After the call ended, Jan picked up a notebook she had pulled from the tote bag she'd received at the festival committee meeting when she'd been drafted into taking charge. "I had a busy day too," she told Elaine, "in addition to the business, I mean."

"What did you do?"

"I checked in with each of my five committee chairmen who are overseeing the various events for the Harvest Home Festival."

"How much work is ahead of you?" Elaine asked. "I hope it's not going to be too stressful."

"A lot of it seems to be under control," Jan reassured her. "All my committee chairs report that their responsibilities are complete or nearly so."

"No glitches so far?"

"A few of the committee heads had questions, but thanks to Hester's amazing notes, I had answers."

"Sounds like everything is going well."

"Not quite everything," Jan admitted. "The scout leader in charge of the corn maze says he hasn't got many of his Boy Scouts lined up to help complete the maze next Thursday evening. I asked if he wanted Dorothy to find him some volunteers, but he said it's handled through the scouts and he'll take care of it. That's the only thing that doesn't seem to be firmed up yet."

"Not bad though," Elaine said. "Thank goodness Hester is the organized sort. Have you gotten any updates on her condition today?"

Jan nodded. "She had surgery to put a plate and pins in her leg. They want to have her up walking soon, but she also sustained a concussion, so they won't release her just yet. She has seventeen stitches over her left forehead and temple."

Elaine winced. "Oh, that sounds terrible. Poor soul. I am praying for her to have a complete recovery." Her cell phone, which she'd set on the arm of the chair, buzzed. Checking the readout, she said, "It's Brody," with a note of surprise in her voice.

CHAPTER EIGHT

Elaine picked up the phone and hit the button to answer the call. "Hi, Brody. How are you?"

She listened a moment. "Um, sure. We're just having a relaxing evening. Come on over." After another moment she said goodbye and set down the phone. "Brody's coming over," she said to Jan.

"What for?"

"I don't know. He didn't say."

Elaine went to her room and exchanged her Ugg slippers for a pair of slip-on shoes before heading downstairs. She had just turned on the front porch light when Brody's big truck growled to a stop in the driveway. Expecting Sasha to be with him, Elaine was puzzled when Brody's tall form got out of the driver's side, but Sasha did not appear.

"Hi!" she called. "Is everything all right?"

Brody's teeth flashed in a broad smile as he approached the porch. A former soldier, Brody still wore his dark hair high and tight in a military cut Elaine knew well. As he removed his cap, she could see he must have had it buzzed recently.

"Everything's fine," he said. "I'm sorry to drop in on you, but I've been thinking, and I wanted to talk to you, and—"

The young man sounded uncharacteristically nervous. Recalling that he'd suffered head trauma during his final deployment, Elaine felt concern rise despite his reassurance. What was going on? "Why don't you come in?" she invited.

Brody followed her into the entryway.

"Would you like a cup of tea?" Elaine asked. "Or coffee? And I'm sure we have something to snack on. Jan's upstairs. Would you like to join us?"

"No, no, I can't stay," Brody said. "It's just that, well, I made all these plans, and then I realized today I hadn't even talked to you." He stopped, took a deep breath, and exhaled. "Mrs. Cook, I want to marry your daughter. Since your husband isn't living, I thought I should speak to you first. Will you give us your blessing if Sasha accepts my proposal?"

Elaine put a hand to her throat, swallowing as she felt tears rise. "Oh, Brody," she said softly. "That's such a thoughtful thing to do." She reached out and covered his hands with hers, stilling the nervous twisting of the hapless cap. "Absolutely, you have my blessing. I will be delighted to welcome you into our family, and I'm sure Jared and his family will say the same thing."

"Whew." Brody let out a long breath of relief. "Thank you." He opened his arms and enveloped Elaine in a hard hug. "Thank you so much. You have no idea how much better I feel. I've been thinking about asking Sasha for a while now, but something just didn't feel quite right—and now I know what it was. Now it's right!"

He stepped back, then pivoted and headed for the door.

"Wait. Are you going to ask her right now?" Elaine asked his back.

Brody stopped and turned, laughing. "No. I guess I seem a little deranged, don't I?"

"Not deranged," Elaine assured him. "Disjointed, maybe?" They both chuckled.

"I'm planning to ask her Thursday evening," he told her. "Will you be home if we come by after?"

Elaine nodded. "Please do. We'll have a little celebration."

She watched as Brody returned to his truck, and then she gently turned off the light and started for the stairs. A wedding to plan! Her footsteps quickened. Jan was going to be so thrilled.

ELAINE ARRIVED AT HMH a few minutes before nine on Wednesday, then parked in front of the building. As she collected her lunch and her handbag, a blue Honda CR-V pulled in beside her. The driver waved merrily before shutting off her engine and hopping out of the small SUV.

"Good morning, Elaine. How are you?"

"Good morning, Sally," Elaine said, recognizing the office manager from downstairs she'd been introduced to yesterday. "I'm good, thanks. How about you?"

"Just fine. I didn't realize until almost closing time yesterday that you're one of the owners of Tea for Two in Lancaster. As soon as I mentioned your name to George—my boss—he recognized it. I guess his wife has brunch there almost weekly."

"Oh my," Elaine said. "I'm sure I know her then."

"I think she's going to be quilting something for a charity auction coming up," Sally said. "Cassie Markham?"

"Oh, of course," Elaine said. "Small world." Her attention was caught by a gorgeous silk scarf Sally had paired with her black trouser suit today. The scarf was lavishly woven with tulips, peonies, and other spring-blooming flowers in pastel shades that practically glowed on the black background. "Your scarf is stunning," Elaine said. "Very unique."

"I got it in Italy," Sally said. "It's vintage, and it's made with real Italian silk. I got it on my last trip there two years ago."

An alarm bell rang in Elaine's mind, amusing her as she recalled Penny's warning from the day before, but it was too late.

"The silk market in northern Italy crashed about forty years ago," Sally told her, "when cheaper Chinese silk flooded the market. Very unfortunate." She took a breath but plunged on before Elaine could get in a word edgewise. "But now that Chinese silk has risen in price, there's a demand for home-grown silk in Italy again, so a number of new factories are opening."

Elaine couldn't resist. "Why has Chinese silk risen in price?"

Sally shrugged. "The biggest reason is a loss of farmland due to rapid industrialization in China. Silkworms require mulberry trees, which require farmland. Did you know silkworms will only eat mulberry leaves? You can see the problem. Chinese raw silk prices have risen over forty percent in the last two years. The Chinese have been stockpiling their silk in anticipation of selling it once the market settles down, but the introduction of artificial fabrics has helped depress the prices."

"How interesting," Elaine said. "I suppose I never thought about where the silk came from."

"Well, there are silkworms in Italy again," Sally said in satisfaction. "In the northern Veneto region, there are a number of factories opening. Where did you say you lived when you were there?"

Elaine smiled and started up the walk as she responded. The pair of them continued to chat as they walked into the main foyer. Sally definitely was more than a little consumed by her interest in Italy.

As they walked into the foyer, Sally pointed out the small rectangular table against the wall. "If you ever come in around eleven, that's where the postman puts the mail for upstairs, and you can take it up with you. Usually Ted comes down and gets it, or I'll take it up if I have time. And every once in a while, Alex will grab it on his way up." Her face fell. "At least, Alex used to. I miss him. I hope they're wrong. I can't imagine that nice man being an embezzler."

Elaine was stunned. The mail was simply left on the table? She said "See you later" to Sally as they parted ways without really even being aware of her actions. *Alex had easy access to the unopened mail*, was all she could think.

Halfway up the stairs, she stopped on the landing. Dan's words from church on Sunday rang in her memory: *Bottom line, you need to check out the other office workers. It almost* has *to be someone who has daily access to incoming checks.*

Or access on days when they suspected there might be lucrative checks being delivered, she thought. If Alex—or someone else—knew when the regular monthly donor checks were likely to arrive, it would be a relatively simple matter to just happen to pick up the mail from the table that day and deliver it to Ted—except for the pertinent donor envelopes, which had been slipped into an inside jacket pocket.

On the other hand, Ted could very well be the embezzler. He would have access to the checks as well as the knowledge of when certain donations were expected. She couldn't rule out R.J, she realized, since she had no idea whether he was privy to any of the donor information. Even Sally appeared to know an awful lot about HMH matters—it was not inconceivable that she could be helping herself to donations.

After climbing to the second floor, Elaine opened the door and entered the HMH foyer, then turned to her left and entered the office suites through Ted's office. He was there already, efficiently faxing something as if he'd never left. The only concrete evidence to prove he'd gone home was that he had on dress pants of a dark navy with his white shirt and today's tie was a deep solid red.

"Good morning, Elaine," he said. "You don't have a time card, so no need to give you my lecture about punching in and out."

"Good morning." Elaine smiled, trying not to think of the possibility that standing in front of her could be a criminal who had set up someone else for his crime.

Ted didn't return the smile. In fact, he merely turned back to the copy/fax machine without another word.

Unsure of what to say to someone who appeared so sober and focused, Elaine quietly passed his desk and walked through the door into the back hallway to the kitchen, where she stowed her lunch in the refrigerator and took her other things to Penny's office.

Penny's office was dark, although the door wasn't locked. Elaine had beaten her there. She hung up her handbag and jacket and headed for the conference room.

Her mind was whirling as it adjusted to the new facts she'd just learned. The mail, oh, the mail. She'd expected her task to be relatively simple after she'd learned that there were only four other employees at HMH. In truth, she'd suspected that Ted probably was the person behind the embezzlement.

But while that still could be true, now she had to face the fact that Alex still had to be considered a suspect, as well as Penny, R.J., and Mitch. And Sally, she supposed, who hadn't even been on her radar.

"Good morning." Mitch stopped in the doorway of the conference room, much as he had yesterday.

"Good morning," Elaine said.

"We can't thank you enough for volunteering to help Penny with this project," the CFO said. "Publicity—favorable publicity, that is—is critical to a nonprofit's success. A mission like ours, building homes, requires a lot of money, and we are always trying to find ways to show the public what we do in an effort to get them to back us."

"I was an army wife," Elaine said, "so I've done my share of volunteering in different organizations around the world. Good publicity is a common denominator in any culture."

"We're going to need some positive events to balance the recent negative coverage." Mitch sighed, his face clouding. "I can't believe this mess with Alex," he said. "I keep thinking it's got to be a mistake. But I can't figure out how it could be."

"You think your CEO's arrest is a mistake?"

Mitch shrugged helplessly. "I don't know what to think. He's a good guy. He loves HMH. But he had company checks hidden in his desk and another in his car. I can't reconcile the two. Maybe if I'd seen it for myself, it would feel more real."

"You weren't here?"

Mitch shook his head. "I was out of the office that day. I come in first thing, but then I'm usually gone for the rest of the day."

Elaine wanted to ask him about what he'd thought when he'd been contacted by the donor who hadn't gotten her tax receipt as she usually did. After all, the woman, Jean Briggs, was a relative of his wife's, wasn't she? But she was deeply aware of how much she knew that she couldn't reveal, so she held her peace.

"Good morning." Penny breezed past the CFO before the silence could grow awkward. "Hi, Mitch. Are you trying to recruit Elaine to help you? Because I saw her first, so you can't have her."

They all laughed, and Mitch snapped his fingers in mock disappointment.

"I'll be right there," Penny said. "Just let me put away my things."

Mitch pushed off the doorway. "Have a good day," he said, "and thanks again for helping."

Penny entered the conference room moments later. "Boy, am I glad to see you. I was afraid maybe I'd scared you off yesterday when you saw how much there is to do."

Elaine chuckled. "I like a challenge."

The two women quickly settled into their routine from the day before, Elaine sorting photos and Penny working on her laptop.

After about ninety minutes, Elaine said, "I think I'll be done sorting the photos that are dated by the end of the day."

"Wow," Penny said. "That's faster than I'd anticipated. So tomorrow, I'll get another laptop for you to use, and we can divide up the ones that aren't dated and start figuring out when, and for what project, they were taken."

"That's going to take some time," Elaine figured. "And then what?"

"Are you familiar with PowerPoint?" Penny asked.

"Oh yes," Elaine said. "I've used it any number of times."

"Great." Penny's eyes lit up. "I thought we could discuss exactly what I have in mind for each of these presentations, and then each of us could take one and start on it."

"Sounds like a good plan," Elaine said. "I can ask your opinion as I go along to make sure I'm sticking with your vision."

Penny laughed. "I suspect your 'vision' will be as clear as my own."

Footsteps in the hallway neared the conference room, and a moment later, Ted stepped inside. "There's a board meeting in here tomorrow," he said, eyeing the piles of photos, the boxes, and the laptop spread around the room.

"That's right," Penny said cheerfully. "Ten to elevenish, isn't it?"

"Yes." Ted appeared to be waiting for something.

Penny smiled at Elaine and returned her attention to her laptop. What was going on here?

Ted cleared his throat. "You'll have to move all these things out and have this room spotless before then, Penny."

Penny looked up, still smiling. "We'll condense it. I'm doing this project at the board's request, so I imagine they'll understand if we're a little space-challenged. We don't have any other place to work on this."

"That won't do," Ted said tightly. "This mess cannot be in here tomorrow."

"It won't be a mess, but it will still be here," Penny said. "I'm sorry, Ted, but that's reality. We use this room for many things, and the board meeting is only one of them."

"It all needs to go," Ted insisted. "The conference room needs to be in tip-top condition before four this afternoon. I have to get it dusted and vacuumed before everyone shows up, so that's the absolute latest you can be in here."

Penny didn't answer. Elaine could see that her expression had altered to one of tight-lipped restraint as she refocused on what she'd been doing, ignoring the office manager.

Ted glared at the top of her head for another moment. Then he swung about and left, his footsteps precise, and returned to his own office.

Penny sighed when they heard the sound of his door closing. "That went well," she said ruefully.

"He's quite insistent about the room being perfect," Elaine observed.

"Everything has to be perfect with Ted," Penny said. "Alex used to intercede and talk him out of some of his worst snits. R.J. ignores him and does what he wants, which makes him mad, and Mitch teases him sometimes, which makes him even more angry. I try to walk a fine line, usually. But one thing I can tell you, we are *not* moving all this stuff. We'll take what we need to work on into my office, and we'll neatly stack the rest in a corner." She glanced around at the boxes. "Can you imagine the two of us and all this stuff in my little closet of an office?"

Elaine looked around and chuckled. "We would be cramped."

They had lunch at the picnic table again, but Sally did not join them. The afternoon passed quickly, and it was three o'clock before Elaine knew where the time had gone.

"We'd better stop," Penny said reluctantly, "and get this stuff organized before Ted comes in here with his dustrag and vacuum at four."

Elaine grinned, making no comment.

She and Penny shut down their work and quickly organized their many piles of photos back into boxes, which they stacked in one corner. Penny strategically moved a potted palm to one side to camouflage the boxes and stepped back. "There. That doesn't look too bad. And it certainly doesn't look messy, does it?"

"Not at all," Elaine assured her. She couldn't imagine that anyone on the board would even notice the discreet stack of boxes and wonder what it was.

"All right," Penny said. "I guess that's all we can do on this for today, so I'm going to spend the last hour and a half on some other things in my office, and you can take off. Will I see you tomorrow?"

"Absolutely," Elaine said. "I'm invested in completing this now." They grinned at each other before Elaine retrieved her belongings and departed.

She drove back to Tea for Two wishing she had accomplished more during the day in terms of information gathering. But she knew she had to step carefully. If Alex was not the embezzler and someone else at Homes for Maine's Heroes had set him up, the last thing she could afford to do was tip off that person to the fact that she was conducting an investigation, even if it was an informal one.

The tearoom was still open when she walked into the kitchen. Rose greeted her and said, "Jan's in the foyer saying goodbye to the last customers."

"Thanks." Elaine walked down the hall to the entryway. Jan was standing near the front door chatting with Rue Maxwell and Macy Atherton.

"Look what the wind blew in," Macy said. "I heard you're a working girl now."

"I'm a working girl here," Elaine said with mock indignation.

"But this is *fun* work," Macy said. "Not like a real job."

Rue snorted. "You're digging a hole you're going to have trouble climbing out of, Macy. Give it up." To Elaine, she said, "Jan told us you're volunteering at Homes for Maine's Heroes. I bet that's an interesting place to be right now."

"What with the embezzling and all," Macy clarified.

"It's had its moments," Elaine admitted.

"I don't know the DeRones," Rue went on, "but everybody says he couldn't have done it. Except I guess they practically caught him red-handed." She paused, clearly hoping Elaine would have details.

"That occurred before I started," Elaine said diplomatically. "I really couldn't say. It's a sad situation though. Everyone is worried that the organization's reputation is going to take a financial hit."

"Oh, with donations, you mean," Macy said. "Well, if that happens, that what's-his-name that works there can just write a check for the difference. What's his name? Married to that richy-rich gal?" She snapped her fingers at Rue for help.

"I don't recall his name," Rue said, "but you're talking about the one married to the Dacourt-Vallerand heiress, right? Only daughter of the two families, worth more than most of the state put together."

"Yeah, that one," Macy said. "Bettina Dacourt-Vallerand. I heard she's a real high-society gal who was spoiled silly by Mommy and Daddy. The story is that they give her pretty much anything she wants, including buying a big ol' house for her and that husband."

"I wonder why he works," Rue mused.

"I imagine he wants to do something constructive," Elaine said, feeling the need to defend the pleasant man she'd spoken with that morning. "He's the chief financial officer, and he's very committed to HMH."

"I guess that's a good fit," Macy decided. "He's got to be used to handling lots of money."

Rue glanced at her watch. "Macy, I've got to go. Are you coming?"

"Ayuh," Macy said. "I have to get dinner started soon. Shane got a deer—you know it's bow season—and I promised to teach Zale my special venison stew recipe that he's always loved." She was speaking of her son and daughter-in-law, Azalea, who ran Green Glade Cottages with her.

But as Macy opened the front door and the pair stepped onto the porch, Elaine heard Macy say, "Well, would ya look at that?"

CHAPTER NINE

Jan and Elaine both craned their necks to peek out the door so they could see whatever had provoked Macy's comment.

Across the street at the Battie house, Realtor Sharon Reddick was replacing the For Sale sign, that had only been there for a week, with an Under Contract sign.

"That was fast," Jan said. "Maybe it was someone who went through it during the Open House on Sunday."

"I wonder who bought it." Macy said as they watched Sharon dump the For Sale sign in the back of her SUV, climb in, and drive away.

"If you don't know, it must be a very well-kept secret," Elaine said, chuckling.

Macy pretended to give her a dirty look, but it was clear that she enjoyed being "in the know" about everything that happened in Lancaster.

"I'll let you know if I hear anything," she promised as she and Rue started down the walk.

"Bye!" Jan called. "Thanks for coming in today." As she and Elaine withdrew into the house, Jan closed and locked the door, then flipped the Open sign over. "We had a decent day today," she said. "People are beginning to get excited about the quilting bee. I had hoped to have a dozen women each at the morning and the afternoon sessions," Jan said, "and every space is filled for each one. Camille's the only repeat who will be at both." Camille, Jan's quilt creator, would be supervising the project and providing the finishing touches once the body of the quilt was completed.

"Wow, that's terrific," said Elaine.

"If it goes as well as I hope, maybe we can make it an annual event. Oh, and did you see what I did today? Probably not," Jan answered her own question. "Because you walked straight to the front door. Turn around."

Elaine did as Jan asked. Their little half-circular pie crust table in the entry had a new look. A basket in the shape of a pumpkin held pens and slips of paper, while a pot of yellow mums bloomed in profusion at one side. At the other side, a big orange pumpkin had been painted with the words, "He or She? What will our little seed be?" and two small mason jars were tied with pink ribbon and blue, and small labels were affixed to them that read He and She. Elaine could see that small slips of paper had already been placed in each jar. A little dish of roasted pumpkin seeds, which appeared to have been depleted by the day's customers already, was the final touch.

At the foot of the table, a display of pumpkins, gourds, a miniature hay bale, and another mum added to the festive look.

"I love it," Elaine declared. "Has Amy seen it?"

Jan shook her head. "No, she probably won't see it until next Wednesday. I'll put out fresh pumpkin seeds each morning between now and then. When the gender-reveal ends, we can easily just convert the table to an autumn display."

"Did you guess yet?" Elaine asked.

Jan grinned. "I was the inaugural guess. Rose and Archie made me go first."

"What did you choose? No, wait, don't tell me." Elaine went to the table and chose a pink pen, which she used to write her name on a slip of paper and crumple it loosely before placing it into the She jar.

Jan laughed in delight. "I chose boy, so one of us will be right either way. I know Amy would be thrilled to get a girl this time, but I don't really care either way. I just can't wait to have a new teeny-weenie to snuggle."

Elaine felt a tiny pang of jealousy, but only a tiny one. "I'll have to live vicariously through you," she said, "until Sasha is ready to have children." She couldn't hide her smile. "Although since Brody's visit last night, I have real hope that someday I may get another grandbaby."

Jan gave her a one-armed hug. "I'm happy to share until then. Living here with you and enjoying each other's families has been one of the best seasons of my life."

Elaine swallowed, touched by the words. "Me too," she said.

Jan released her after a final squeeze. "I've got to make some more cranberry scones," she said.

BACK IN THE kitchen, Jan assembled the ingredients for the cranberry scones that had become a customer favorite since she'd first tested them a year ago.

She cut the butter and dry ingredients into pea-sized pieces. Then, mixing in cranberries, sugar, and orange rind, she stirred until the ingredients were well blended. The phone began to ring just as she poured the buttermilk-egg mixture into the main body of the batter. As she started to mix with slow, steady strokes, she clicked to answer, hit speaker, and said, "Hello?"

"Hi, Jan. It's Camille. Have you got all the quilt blocks together yet?"

"Hi, Camille. I will after about ten tomorrow morning," Jan told her. "I know you wanted to have time to figure out how best to arrange the blocks, so I can drop them by tomorrow after the tearoom closes at four if you like."

"That would be wonderful," Camille said. "We can lay them all out together and see how they look, and maybe come up with a tentative arrangement. I always like to let them sit for a day or so and then decide if I want to make any changes before I start stitching them together. Another set of eyes is always welcome."

"That would be great. If Elaine is free, may I bring her along?"

"Absolutely."

After a few more moments of conversation, Jan ended the call. She made a large, soft ball with the buttermilk dough, kneaded it about a dozen times, and divided it into four equal balls. She patted each piece into a circle about an inch thick and placed them on an ungreased cookie sheet.

As she scored each ball into quarters so she could easily cut them into four equal pieces later, Elaine came into the kitchen. Taking a look at what Jan was doing, she said, "Yum. Your cranberry scones are one of my favorite recipes ever."

Then she took a closer look at the cookie sheet. "You only made sixteen?"

Jan smiled. "I want to have some ready for first thing in the morning. When Rose gets here, she can make another batch—or two—if we need them."

"If we have another day like you had today, you may need two more batches," Elaine said. "I just looked at the receipts. When you said it was a good day, I didn't realize you meant it was a Goooood Daaaaayyy." She nodded as she drew out the last two words.

Jan chuckled. "Yes. I was pleased. Even though the summer tourists have gone, we seem to be holding our own with business." She opened the oven, popped in the tray of scones, and set the timer for seventeen minutes. The recipe called for twenty, but she had found her oven always baked them a little dry if she gave them the full time.

"What would you like for dinner?" Elaine asked.

Jan shrugged. "I'm feeling flexible tonight."

"I've been hungry for fish tacos all week. How does that sound?"

"Terrific." Jan flashed her cousin a grin. "Especially if you're making them."

"That was my plan," Elaine agreed. While she chopped, fried, and assembled an assortment of dishes for the meal, she gave Jan a quick rundown of the day. "I certainly didn't find a smoking gun," she said. "Ted seems to be a little demanding, but that's hardly the same as being guilty of embezzlement."

"You learned that a lot of people have access to the mail before it gets to the office upstairs," Jan pointed out. "That could be significant. Maybe tomorrow will bring something new to light," she added. "We can't expect the answer to just fall into our laps. This is a whole different type of investigation from just poking around informally looking into something. This time, we've been *asked* to investigate." She couldn't hide the pride in her tone.

Elaine laughed. "Yes, we have. And now my major concern is that we won't be able to deliver. What if we can't find the answer?" She hesitated a moment. "Or even worse, what if we find out that Alex DeRone really did embezzle from HMH? Even if Dan didn't blame us for confirming it, you know it will throw a shadow over our friendship forever."

"I keep wondering if Alex has been framed," Jan said. "Especially since you found that letter he wrote to the editor about his predecessor's overly large salary. He was certainly opposed to rewarding executives with outsized salaries at the time."

"And since we know his own salary is far more modest," Elaine added, nodding. "But have his ideals changed that much for the worse in just a few years? He felt strongly enough to write that letter, so what changed? Or, as you wonder, has he been framed?"

THURSDAY MORNING, ELAINE again arrived at Homes for Maine's Heroes on the dot of nine. Sally's car was not in the parking lot yet, but there were several other cars parked near the door that likely belonged to the HMH staff.

Ted was already in the office. "Board meeting this morning," he reminded her. "You and Penny will have to work in her office."

"We're prepared to do that," Elaine responded.

Penny was coming in behind her, so Elaine went on down the hallway and hung up her jacket and handbag. They had decided to go out for lunch today, so Elaine hadn't packed anything to put in the refrigerator. "Good morning," she said as Penny came into her small office.

"Morning." Penny made a face. "I was in a good mood until Ted got in a little dig about the conference room."

"Oh well," Elaine said. "We'll make this work. It's only for a couple of hours."

"I borrowed you a laptop, anyway," Penny said, "and I brought one box of the undated pictures in here, so we can keep working on getting all of those dated."

"Sounds good," Elaine said.

R.J. paused in Penny's doorway a few minutes later. "Good morning, ladies."

"Morning, R.J.," Penny said. "What are you up to today?"

"Going out to check on a building site this morning," he said, "and light a little fire under the project manager." He chuckled. "And this afternoon, I have meetings with two architects who have developed designs for a couple of new home plans we're considering. How about you?"

"Still working on organizing these photos and getting PowerPoints together," Penny said.

Mitch stuck his head in the doorway. "Man, I wish I were any one of you this morning. I hate board meetings."

R.J. laughed. "And I'm glad you're not me. I have enough trouble with the building committee meetings."

"Building." Mitch screwed up his handsome features in an expression of distaste. "After Bettina and I get finished with the house, I do not ever want to see another blueprint, paint sample, tile chip, or anything to do with building or decorating again."

"Are you close?" Penny asked. To Elaine, she said, "Mitch and his wife are finishing building a home on Messalonskee Lake."

"More like a mansion," R.J. said. "You're going to rattle around a 4600-square-foot house."

Mitch turned both palms up, grinning. "Never argue with a woman. What the wife wants, the wife gets. And even a house that big won't be quiet with the kids around." He smiled fondly. "Man, I wish I could freeze them at this age. Kids grow up too fast."

"How old are your children?" Elaine asked.

"Three and almost five," Mitch told her, his face lighting up. "Both girls."

"I really enjoyed the years before my son and daughter started school," Elaine said. "I know what you mean. It would be wonderful if they could stay those ages."

"It would." Mitch glanced at his watch. "Yikes. Gotta go finish printing out my reports. Have a good day, everyone. Wish me luck at the board meeting."

"Luck!" they all chorused. Elaine waved, enjoying the camaraderie.

"He adores those little girls," Penny said, smiling.

"Kids are the best," R.J. said. "My grands make my world brighter, that's for sure." He peeled away a moment later, heading into his own office. Shortly afterward, Mitch bustled down the hall with a sheaf of papers beneath one arm and they heard the door to the conference room open and close.

As the pair booted up their laptops and began to work identifying photos, they could hear noise from the end of the hall closest to Ted's office, where the board members were congregating for their meeting. Ted could be heard greeting people, directing them into the conference room, and offering coffee.

"Don't forget," Penny said. "Find some excuse to go into Ted's office at eleven, right after the mail arrives. You have to see Ted in action."

Elaine was eager to do exactly that. "I'll try to do it today."

Just then, there was the sound of raised, panicked voices and commotion in the hallway.

"Call 9-1-1!" someone shouted.

CHAPTER TEN

Penny and Elaine both set aside their laptops and hurried into the hallway.

A man sat on the floor near the conference room door. Mitch was in front of him, and Ted knelt at one side. "We're getting help, Mr. Burgess," Mitch said. He looked at the people standing around. "What happened?"

"We were in the conference room talking about the embezzlment," a woman in a navy suit said. "He grabbed the back of the chair like he was dizzy and then staggered to the door. He leaned against the frame and just sort of slid to the floor."

"What's wrong?" Penny asked.

"I don't know." Mitch sounded a little desperate.

The man on the floor tried to say something, but Elaine couldn't understand him. Instantly, she had a suspicion. She stepped forward and knelt at the man's other side. "Sir," she said, "can you smile at me?"

The man on the floor looked older than she by perhaps a decade. His eyes were wide and frightened as they fixed on her, and she repeated her request. When he tried to comply, she saw that one side of his face drooped and did not respond as the other side did.

"Good, that's good," she said reassuringly. "Can you raise your arms for me and hold them out at shoulder level?"

He raised both arms—and one drifted back down to his side. He tried to speak, but Elaine couldn't understand what he was trying to say.

"Any dizziness, sir?" That was Mitch.

Again, the man said something, but Elaine still couldn't understand what he said.

"Ask him to repeat a sentence," Elaine said urgently. "A simple one."

Mitch hesitated a moment and then asked, "Mr. Burgess, repeat this sentence: The cow jumped over the moon."

"Thaaa caaaa—" The rest of the sentence deteriorated into something so garbled Elaine couldn't understand it.

Ted was firing directions at another man standing nearby on his cell phone, apparently on the line with a 9-1-1 dispatcher. He had already given the address of HMH when Ted said, "Tell them to hurry!"

"Tell them," Elaine said, "he may be having a stroke."

The man promptly relayed the information. He turned to the group and said, "They're on their way. Should be here within a few minutes. The station's not far."

"I'll go downstairs and wait for the EMTs," Elaine volunteered. "It might go faster if I flag them down."

"Good idea. Thanks."

As Elaine rushed through Ted's office and the foyer and began to descend the steps, she could already hear sirens, and she quickened her steps.

Sally came to the door of the brokerage firm. "What's going on?"

"Board member having a stroke," Elaine said, yanking open the exterior door and then hurrying to stand outside.

"Oh no." Sally hurried after her. "Who?"

"Mr. Burgess," Elaine said. "The board president."

"Oh no." Sally jumped up and down, waving her arms as an emergency vehicle with flashing lights and siren turned into the main entry of the office complex. "Back here!" she called, as if they could hear her. "Hurry!"

An hour later, things had settled down in the office. Mr. Burgess had been taken to the hospital. After a brief shell-shocked period where everyone had stood around and discussed when they had begun to notice something wasn't right, the board members drifted out. The vice president of the board made a comment about rescheduling the meeting, since it was clear no one had the heart for it just now.

R.J. had gone off to his meetings, and Mitch, Ted, Penny, and Elaine had put the lobby and the front office back in order—some of the furniture was askew from the EMTs moving it to get a stretcher through. Shortly afterward, Mitch left to go by the hospital and then attend some afternoon meetings.

When Elaine glanced at the clock again, it was almost eleven. She wondered if Ted's mail routine would be upset by the incident in the office. Perhaps this was as good a time as any to find out.

Rising from her seat at the laptop, Elaine said, "It's almost eleven. I think I'll go ask Ted to make me a copy of this photo, just for reference, even though it won't be good quality."

A spark of humor lit Penny's eyes. "Good idea."

Elaine walked to Ted's office just a few yards down the hall. As she paused in the doorway, Ted came in from the foyer door with a stack of envelopes in his hand.

"I was wondering if—" she began.

Ted brushed aside her words. "It'll have to wait until I've done this mail." While Elaine continued to stand in the doorway, he went around his desk, sat in his chair, and proceeded to restack the handful of mail. He sorted it by size, smallest envelopes on top, largest on the bottom, and then carefully aligned it so the left and bottom corners matched.

As Elaine watched in bemusement, Ted laid the newly organized stack on his desk while he pulled out a ledger, a slim silver letter opener, and a pen. He then turned and very precisely positioned those items on the credenza behind him, faced his desk again, and picked up the mail. He turned his back to Elaine and laid the mail on the credenza. Then, without ever acknowledging that Elaine was still there, the office manager proceeded to open each piece of mail.

Ted hunched over his work almost protectively. He appeared to sort the mail into several piles. Catalogs in one, she could see, but the others were anyone's guess. Invoices? Donations? Other correspondence?

Next, he took one pile that was directly in front of him and proceeded to pull out the contents, make a note in a ledger, and set them aside. He pulled a second pile toward him and did the same thing. He didn't extract the contents of a third pile. Those he placed on top of the stack of catalogs. Then he picked up the other two stacks and turned around.

"Oh," he said, "you're still here."

"I'd like to use the copier," she said.

"Just give me one moment to deliver these to Mitch's office," he said, "and I'll show you how it works."

Elaine was pretty certain that she could figure out how to make one black-and-white copy, but she nodded. "Sure." And now she knew that Ted was the first person to open and record all the incoming donations. Presumably, he would be in the prime position to spirit away a check without ever recording it.

She wanted to take a look at the other pieces of mail left on the credenza, but it was on the far side of Ted's desk, and she wouldn't have any good explanation for what she was doing back there if he caught her, so she resisted.

The phone rang, and she heard Ted's rapid rush along the hallway back to the office. She was glad she hadn't rounded that desk.

In a hurry, he reached across his desk and picked up the receiver. "Homes for Maine's Heroes. This is Ted. How may I help you?" A moment later, he said, "What? Have you told R.J.? Yes, I know he's in meetings…All right, I'll try to get hold of him and I'll check with the company." Hanging up the phone, he shook his head. "One project manager says the lumber company didn't deliver enough of the pressure-treated wood they ordered for the deck they're putting on, and the company says they did. And R.J. is out of touch. As usual," he said with a sniff.

He bustled over to the copy machine. "Here," he said, lifting the lid, "is how you place your paper on the glass." After a few quick taps of buttons and accompanying instructions, he said, "and voilà, there's your copy."

"Thanks," Elaine said. The phone rang again, and she lingered. Who knew what scrap of information might be important?

Ted glanced at the readout, then reached for the phone and hit speaker. "R.J. Why haven't you answered Cameron's calls?"

"I was in a meeting." R.J.'s voice echoed around the office. "I didn't even see he'd called until just now. Do you—?"

"Well, you need to call him back right away," Ted said. "And call the lumber people and tell them they made a mistake."

"I don't have a lot of time here," R.J. said, sounding exasperated. "I just stepped out of the meeting for a minute. Can you please call about the wood? Just ask them to send whatever we were short, and I'll figure out who made the error and how to fix it later. We've got to get that deck done—we're barely managing to stay on deadline. We have a start date of November first for the next house, so we've got to get this one completed."

"It's not my job to fix your project problems," Ted said. "I have quite a few things on my plate today already."

"But I'm telling you that I literally can't get to it," R.J. said in tones that suggested he was struggling to hang on to his patience. "Will you please make the phone call? As I recall, much of your job description has to do with supporting those of us who are working directly with the building teams and fund-raisers. If you think that just because we don't have a CEO or a board president right now you can slack off, then you can think again, son."

"I am not your son," Ted said tightly. "But because I am a team player, I will make that call. After that, you can clean up your own mess." Angrily, he stabbed at the button to end the call.

Then he laid both palms flat on the desk before him, closed his eyes, and drew in a deep, slow breath before releasing it and opening his eyes. As he focused on Elaine, he frowned. "Did you need something else?" It appeared he had forgotten she still was standing there.

"I only wanted to ask if you needed me to let you know any time I use the copier," she improvised, a little stunned by how the phone call had blown up into an angry exchange. "I doubt it will be frequent, but I want to be sure I follow company policy."

Ted waved a hand. "No special rules. I thought we should have a sheet by the copier for everyone to fill in their initials and number of copies made, but Alex said we're so small he didn't feel it was necessary at this time." He sounded aggrieved by Alex's response.

Elaine couldn't help but wonder...was Ted aggrieved enough to frame the CEO for embezzlement? A copier sign-in was a small detail, but Ted seemed to have a lot of anger inside him.

She wasn't really sure what to say in response. "I imagine this is a very stressful time for all of you. I hope things will settle down soon," she said, trying for diplomacy.

"Me too," Ted said. "I'm tired of feeling like everyone's whipping boy."

Elaine wasn't sure she agreed with that assessment. Recalling Ted's skirmish with Penny yesterday and now seeing how he'd responded to R.J., Elaine thought he could be a little more flexible with his coworkers.

"As far as I can see, everyone here has a very important job," Elaine said honestly. "It takes all of you to keep things moving in the right direction."

"That's exactly what I mean," Ted said. "No one around here appreciates the work it takes to keep track of all the things everyone is involved in. They think all I do is answer phones and forward messages."

"I'm sure that's not true," Elaine said. "An organization is only as efficient as its front office. From what I've seen, you do an excellent job."

"Thank you." Ted's ruffled feathers appeared to be settling back into place. "I guess I'll make that phone call on R.J.'s behalf now."

Back in Penny's office, Elaine closed the door.

Penny looked up with a grin. "You were in there a while. Get an eyeful?"

"And an earful," Elaine said honestly. "Ted seems a little... stressed out. I feel bad for him."

"He causes half of his own troubles," Penny said, "by being so 'my way or the highway.' On my nicer days, I try to be sympathetic to his need for order, but sometimes he just gets on my last nerve." Penny sighed. "Anyway, so you saw the mail routine. The ordering of the envelopes by size, the careful corners, the separating into whatever piles he deems important...it's quite a ritual, isn't it?"

"It is," Elaine agreed. Getting back to work on her borrowed laptop, she let the conversation lapse. But in her mind's eye, she saw Ted organizing the mail, separating it according to some system, recording what she suspected were checks and invoices.

If Alex wasn't the HMH embezzler, then Ted very well could be. But why would Ted steal money from the company? Was he in debt? Did he gamble or have some other expensive vice? She hadn't even known any of the HMH office staff for a week yet, except for Penny, so she just didn't know. She was going to have to try to discover more about Ted, she realized. He certainly had the best opportunity—

But he didn't, necessarily. She remembered the "mail table" in the entry foyer at the foot of the steps. If Sally was correct about the many people who had the opportunity to bring the mail upstairs, any number of people could be the one spiriting away a check here, a check there—Alex being as likely as any of them.

Even Sally herself, Elaine realized, could be embezzling from HMH. She would be the last one under suspicion, since she didn't even work for the company. But it also had to be someone with access to Alex's office to plant the checks in his desk, she reminded herself. Could Sally have managed that? Elaine had to force herself not to let her mind wander from the project she was working on. She couldn't wait to discuss all the information she had with Jan later.

Since the board meeting was not going to be held, after they returned from lunch Elaine and Penny moved their things back to the conference room, where they could spread out again, and resumed work.

Around one thirty, they heard Ted welcoming someone into the front office. A deep male voice murmured something they didn't catch, and then Ted said, "Yes, sir. Of course. You can use the CEO's office since it's empty." He sounded more than a little unnerved, and Penny and Elaine shared a look of concern.

Before either of them could rise, Ted came by the door of the conference room, followed by two men. They were state troopers, Elaine saw instantly, just like Dan Benson. Ted paused in the doorway and gave Penny a sickly smile. "These gentlemen are here to ask us a few more questions. They'll start with me and then talk to you and Mitch." To the troopers, he indicated Elaine, saying, "Elaine is a volunteer who is helping us out just for this week, so I doubt you'll want to talk to her."

Then he proceeded down the hallway with the police officers behind him.

Both women watched them move out of sight.

"What do you think they want?" Penny whispered.

Elaine shrugged. "I imagine they probably just want to review what you've already told them and possibly ask a few more questions."

Several minutes later, Ted came down the hallway. "Your turn," he said to Penny. "In Alex's office."

Penny swallowed and rose. "Back in a little while," she said to Elaine.

She was gone only a short time, but when she returned, she looked distinctly shaken.

Elaine didn't even have to ask what happened.

"They questioned me about Alex," Penny said. "Did I know if he had ever borrowed money from Homes for Maine's Heroes. I said no, of course." Then she looked uncertain. "I think they're trying to track down some kind of payment to Alex. But I don't know of anything Alex would have done outside of his normal salary that he'd have needed to be paid for."

"So, they really believe they have their man." Elaine didn't know what else to say. "I wonder what they know that the public doesn't, to make them so sure."

Penny bit her lip. "Elaine, I'm pretty sure I know why the police suspect Alex."

"Why?"

"One of the troopers told me that the check found in Alex's car was a company-issued check that Alex wrote to himself."

Elaine was flabbergasted. "To himself?"

Penny nodded, and tears welled in her eyes. "I just can't believe he'd do that. But apparently it was for $15,000."

"Does anyone else know?"

"I don't know," Penny said. "I haven't mentioned it to the others. I don't want it to be true. I'm not sure if the troopers asked anyone else about it. They told me to keep it quiet, but I just had to talk to someone."

That answered one question Elaine might have asked. Her heart sank as she recalled what Dan had said about the prosecutors wanting to make the sentence as large as possible based on the amount of money they thought Alex had embezzled. Obviously, the investigators were trying to figure out that check they had found in Alex's car. She was pretty curious about it as well. What could he possibly have been thinking, making out a check from HMH to himself?

A little while later, Penny sent Elaine to Ted's office to ask him for some large paper clips. To her surprise, the normally efficient office manager was sitting at his desk with his head in his hands.

CHAPTER ELEVEN

As the office manager sat with his hands cradling his head, Elaine was surprised to see that on his left wrist, Ted wore a large gold watch with a handsome blue enamel face. She recognized it instantly because she had given Ben one for their twentieth wedding anniversary. Squinting, she looked at the brand name displayed on the face. Yes, it was indeed a Rolex.

Ted slowly dropped his hands when he heard her come in.

"Ted, what's wrong?" She didn't have to fake the concern in her voice. The young man looked weary and upset.

"I'm just worried," he said. "Those officers upset me. HMH is such a worthwhile organization, and we have a really good team of employees. They made me feel like...oh, I don't know. Like we're all suspicious characters who shouldn't be handling people's donations."

"They upset Penny too." Elaine didn't tell him that they'd asked specifically about Alex borrowing money.

"Alex is a good man. I just can't believe he would have stolen money from this organization. He must have needed it really, really badly if he did, but I'm not saying I believe it." He shook his head, straightening his cuffs and returning his watch to its hiding place beneath his sleeve.

She wanted another look at that watch. It cost thousands, if she was correct. Where on earth had Ted Harrington gotten the money for such a watch?

That was the problem. For all she knew, Ted could be as wealthy as Mitch Ackerly and his wife. She had to figure out a way to get to know more about him. Impulsively, she said, "You know my cousin and I run Tea for Two in Lancaster, right?"

Ted nodded. "Penny mentioned it. It sounds like something my mother would have loved."

His mother wasn't living? Elaine filed that away to examine later. "We're completing a quilt to auction off at the Chickadee Lake Harvest Home Festival. Have you ever been to it?"

Ted shook his head. "I've heard it's a wonderful event, full of all kinds of interesting traditional activities."

"Why don't you come this year?" Elaine asked. "It's coming up a week from Saturday."

"I can't," Ted said, and she was sure she heard a note of regret in his voice. "I spend every Saturday with my mother."

"How lovely. Until recently, both of my children lived out of the area, so I didn't get to see them often. I'm sure your mother cherishes your visits."

Ted smiled, but it looked pained. "Sometimes it is lovely." He reached for a silver-framed photo on his desk and turned it around so Elaine could see a tiny, white-haired woman in a wheelchair. She looked off to one side, unsmiling, as if she was unsure of herself.

"My mother has early-onset Alzheimer's," he said. "She's only about your age, but she's been in a nursing home for two years now after I couldn't keep her at home any longer."

"Oh, Ted," Elaine said softly. "I am so sorry. That's a difficult disease."

He nodded matter-of-factly. "It is. She still recognizes me every once in a while, but most of the time she doesn't. She really comes alive when I sing to her though. She sang to me all the time when I was a child, so now I sing all those old songs we used to enjoy. It seems to comfort her when she's agitated."

"How long did you have her at home once she was diagnosed?" Elaine asked.

"Not quite three years," Ted said. "It progressed rapidly, and she had episodes where she would wander off and forget what she was doing. One day she went into the neighbor's house and took a nap in their bed and tried to cook. They were out working in their garden, and they came in to find her starting to make bacon and eggs for 'breakfast.' She made a huge mess. They were quite kind about it, but that was when I realized I couldn't leave her alone anymore."

"Where is she living?" Elaine was familiar with a number of the elder-care facilities in the central Maine area, since many of her mother's friends were downsizing and some were moving into retirement and care communities.

"She's in the dementia unit at Blueberry Run," he told her. "It's costly, but she deserves the best. My father died when I was very young, and she worked hard to keep a roof over our heads and give me every advantage she could." He picked up a pile of neatly stacked papers and nervously tapped the edges to align them perfectly. "She's very special to me."

"I can tell," Elaine said. "I think it's wonderful that you take such good care of her."

"I wish I could have her at home," he said wistfully. "But getting private nursing care was even more costly than residential living, and you have to be so careful to make sure you get good people, and really, how would I know, since I can't be there? I am terrified she might not be treated well."

"I'm sure it was a very difficult decision," Elaine said, "but it speaks volumes that you have your mother's best interests in mind. My mother has a friend whose husband is at Blueberry Run, and she's been very happy with his care there." Although, Elaine recalled, she talked incessantly about how expensive it was. Which raised the question of how Ted afforded such an expense *and* a Rolex.

"She has to be safe," Ted said. "And well cared for and stimulated, to try to keep her from losing ground any faster."

"It sounds like you made an excellent choice," Elaine assured him, setting aside her thoughts for later consideration.

As she returned to the conference room to resume her task with Penny, she felt sympathy for the young man. He clearly cared deeply for his mother and was distressed by her deterioration. Having known a few people with family members living with Alzheimer's, Elaine felt terribly sad for him. It was a horrible, heartbreaking disease that affected family members as much as it did the afflicted person, albeit in different ways. She wondered if Ted's obsession for things being "just so" at the office was a coping mechanism to help him deal with the things in his life that he couldn't control. And she wondered exactly what lengths the young man would go to in order to give his mother the best care possible.

The workday ended. Penny was meeting her husband and some friends for dinner at a local Italian place and she invited Elaine to come along. "You could call Jan too."

Elaine chuckled. "Jan's pretty crazed with preparations for Harvest Home. We'd love to join you, but perhaps another time would be better."

Each woman gathered her things. After parting from Penny in the parking lot, Elaine headed home. What a day. She couldn't wait to tell Jan everything she'd learned.

The tearoom had closed, but Rue Maxwell still was there, standing in the front hallway talking with Jan when Elaine walked in to hang up her coat.

"Hi, Elaine." Jan and Rue both turned to face her as Rue spoke.

"Hi, Rue. Hi, Jan. Good day?"

"Steady," Jan said, "although we weren't overwhelmed."

"The food and tea were excellent, as usual," Rue told her.

"I've got a little problem with the festival committee,' Jan said, "and Rue is going to help me."

"Oh? What's wrong?"

"I was just telling Rue that I have called this scoutmaster who's in charge of the corn maze three times and left messages, and the man hasn't called me back yet. I need to confirm that he's prepared to have his scouts there next Thursday evening to put the finishing touches on the maze before the festival on Saturday."

Rue was frowning too. "He's my neighbor. I've known him for years. So I told Jan I'd try to give him a nudge and remind him there is a time constraint here. After all, the festival is just over a week away."

"Exactly," Jan said. "I'll be in your debt if you can get him to call me back. My only other option is to just show up at his house."

"I'll give it my best shot," Rue promised. "I'll tell him you need to hear from him by Saturday since you're shorthanded with the planning."

"Thanks." After Rue departed, Jan closed and locked the door. "I hope your day was more fruitful than mine."

"My day," Elaine announced, "was chock-full of information. I haven't even had a chance to process it all yet."

"Do tell. No, wait, you'll have to tell me later. Camille would like us to come over and help her with a tentative layout for the quilt, now that I finally have all the quilt blocks."

"That's exciting," Elaine said. "I can't wait to see them all."

Camille only lived two blocks away, so the cousins walked over.

CAMILLE AND HER husband lived in a rancher of warm beige siding with soft green shutters built on a slight slope with an attached garage set down a few feet from the house proper.

"Come on in," she invited, pulling open the door as the cousins ascended the steps to the deck that fronted the house.

In the workroom, two sewing tables with large, sophisticated sewing machines stood against one wall, while an enormous worktable was the focus of the room. An ironing board stood nearby, and floor-to-ceiling cabinets lined another wall.

"Oh my goodness," Jan said. "This is my dream come true. What an amazing room."

Camille smiled. "It was a big unfinished space when we bought the house, and it's been perfect for my little sewing obsession."

Both cousins laughed.

"I totally get that," Jan said.

"So here are the quilt blocks you collected. Did you bring the other two?" Camille indicated the colorful autumn-themed fabric pieces on the table.

Jan nodded. "Sure did." She withdrew the two squares from her bag that she had rolled up after ironing them. She unrolled the fabric tube, then smoothed out each square and passed it to Camille.

The quilter laid them on the table with the other finished pieces. She had a large swatch of the background fabric beneath them so the trio could see how the completed color arrangement would look. "I laid the rest out in what I thought was a pleasing arrangement, but depending on how the two newest ones look, we may have to move some things around." She pulled all the pieces into alignment, and then the three women stood back and studied it.

"Too much orange in this corner," Camille said. "Do you agree?"

Jan nodded. She walked around the table and pointed to a motif of a golden corn shock. "Let's switch this one with that one." She pointed to the one she had made.

Camille scooped up the block while Jan did the same, and when the switch had been made, they studied it again.

"Much better," Jan opined.

Elaine cleared her throat. "Color-wise, it's much more evenly distributed. But now you have three blocks with autumn leaves all down here in this corner." When both of the other women turned to look at her, she trailed off uncertainly. "But maybe that doesn't matter as long as the colors work."

"It does matter," Camille said. "If we'd gone with this arrangement, that would have bugged me for days once I noticed it. And I *would* have noticed it eventually, so thank you."

"What if we switch this one"—Jan pointed to a trio of gourds—"with the one of the leaves spilling out of the basket?"

"Oh yes," Camille agreed. "The colors are similar, and it would be enough to break up the leaf-heavy corner."

Elaine was closest to the leaves, so she and Jan switched the two blocks. Once again, they all studied the layout.

"All right." Camille dusted off her hands to show that they were done tinkering. "I'll get it stitched together. You open at ten next Wednesday, right?" When Jan nodded, she went on. "I'll arrive around nine thirty then, with the frame and the quilt sandwich ready to be quilted."

"Quilt sandwich?" Elaine raised her eyebrows.

Jan grinned. "That's what we call an assembled quilt top, batting, and backing that haven't been quilted together yet. The edges are raw because the border is the last thing to be finished, and the three layers are basted or held together with nonrusting safety pins."

"It almost seems as if we should serve a 'quilt sandwich special' that day."

Jan and Camille both laughed.

"That's a great idea," Jan said. "I'll add it to the list."

"Put me down for one," Camille said, still chuckling.

As the cousins were walking home a few minutes later, Jan's cell phone rang. She pulled it from her pocket and, seeing the display, she said, "It's Rue." She raised the phone to her ear.

"Hi, Rue, what's up?" After a short conversation, Jan ended the call and replaced the phone in her pocket. "Rue says she saw her neighbor and asked him about the corn maze, and he went into a song and dance about good help being hard to come by. I think I'm going to drive over there and talk to him face-to-face as soon as we get back. Then I need to make a stop at the store for a few things I need for tomorrow."

Elaine nodded. "Sounds like you'd better get a handle on the maze problem. How about I make us a quiche for dinner while you're gone?"

"That sounds terrific," Jan said. "Any special kind?"

"What kind do you have a taste for?"

"That broccoli, cheddar, and bacon quiche you made last time was fantastic, and I know we have all those ingredients." Jan smacked her lips.

Elaine grinned. "Then that's what it'll be."

While Elaine went to the kitchen to begin assembling her quiche, Jan grabbed her purse and keys and headed for her blue Toyota.

It took only minutes to drive over to the cottage just past Rue and Ned Maxwell's bed-and-breakfast, Northwoods B&B.

Turning the Tables

Jan parked in the driveway of the deep-red Cape Cod-style home with its white shutters and walked up the flagstone path. Standing on the front stoop, she rang the doorbell and waited until the door opened. A thin man with thick glasses that made his hazel eyes look enormous peered out. "Yes?"

"Hi. Mr. Vermeyer?" At his quick nod, she said, "I'm Jan Blake, the stand-in coordinator for the festival. Rue Maxwell said you're having some trouble with volunteers for the corn maze, and since I was in the area, I thought I'd stop and talk to you directly."

"Please come in," the scoutmaster said.

Jan followed him into a pleasant front room and took the seat he indicated on an oatmeal-colored couch with teal-and-beige striped throw cushions.

The man took a seat on a striped chair across from her and said, "I'm kind of in a bind, Mrs. Blake. I kept thinking I'd be able to find someone, so I put off calling you back, but the truth is I haven't found the help I need. All my Eagle Scouts have graduated except for one, and there's a dearth of younger scouts as well."

"I thought the maze was preplanned and grown from scratch each summer," Jan said. "What remains to be done?"

Mr. Vermeyer sighed. "It's true that the maze is designed and planted early in July, and we did manage to get that done. We use a special tall corn variety and plant the stalks close for dense walls. However, even though the paths are essentially in place, there's still a lot of work to be done at the last minute."

Jan was taking notes in the festival notebook she had brought along. "Give me a list."

Jan began to scribble as the man spoke, writing down *straw for paths, signs for entrance and exit,* and *tower.*

"A tower?" Jan could not recall ever going through the maze, and she wasn't sure what he meant.

"We erect a tower in the center. There's always a lookout posted there when the maze is open to assist lost people inside the maze, keep an eye out for children who get separated from their parents, and call for help in the event of a medical emergency. I keep the lumber, ladder, and platforms from year to year, but it still takes time to erect it." Mr. Vermeyer's worried look eased for a moment. "The good news is that plenty of people have signed up to take look-out shifts during the festival. A lot of the same people volunteer for that from year to year. It's just the Thursday night final setup that I'm having trouble with."

"All right. I'll see if I can find some folks to give us a hand," Jan promised, rising. Thanking the scoutmaster for his time, Jan took her leave and headed for the store.

Elaine's quiche was in the oven as Jan walked in with her sacks of groceries. After putting away the things she'd bought, Jan set the table while she reported what she had learned. "I guess I'll have to call the volunteer coordinator," she said, "and see if she can round me up a couple of people."

The timer went off, and Elaine removed the quiche from the oven and set it on a large hot pad in the center of the table. She also had cut up and cored a fresh pineapple, and she quickly removed spears of asparagus in melted butter from a skillet on the stove and placed them in a serving dish.

"Dinner smells great."

"Almost ready," Elaine said, setting the asparagus and a set of serving tongs on the table.

Jan slid into her seat just as Elaine did. Elaine offered a blessing, and then the cousins began to eat.

"So, I want to hear everything about your day," Jan said.

Elaine shook her head. "It was a doozy. Where do I start?"

CHAPTER TWELVE

After recapping the day for Jan, Elaine said, "That mail table downstairs is a problem. Anyone who knows about when the mail is to be delivered could steal a few envelopes without anyone being the wiser."

"Until they get tripped up by alert donors like that Jean Briggs, who don't get their tax-record letters," Jan pointed out.

"I've been thinking about that," Elaine said. "Whoever pulled off this embezzlement knew something about how to cover it up. I suspect he or she knows who the big-money donors are and when their checks come in. They pull those and send out thank-you letters for tax purposes on company letterhead, and no donors are the wiser."

"Yet somehow the embezzler messed up in the case of Jean Briggs."

"Yes," Elaine allowed. "And I have another suspect to add to our list."

"Who's that?"

"Sally in the office downstairs."

Jan's eyes rounded. "Because she also has access to the mail. In fact, you said her office door is glass, right? She could see the mailman arrive and be out there within seconds."

Elaine nodded.

"But it would do her no good unless she knew who the big donors were and the timing of their giving," Jan pointed out.

"True."

"I'd think that would be fairly easy to discover," Jan said. "Nonprofits are always thanking their donors. Some of them even publish lists in their newsletters."

"You're right." Elaine looked crestfallen. "This is getting harder, not easier. I thought I'd be able to eliminate some people after a few days at the office. Instead, we're adding names to our list."

Elaine went on to tell Jan about her conversation with Ted and the information about his mother's costly care.

Jan whistled. "Hello, motive." She thought for a moment. "Tell me more about the project coordinator. You haven't spoken about him much."

Elaine shrugged. "There's nothing specific, but R.J. does have the opportunity, being in and out of the office daily." Then she frowned. "There was an issue today...he got into it with Ted. Something about a company not delivering enough lumber to a job site, although the company says they did. He asked Ted to call them about it, and he said he'd figure it out later. If I were a really suspicious type of person, I might wonder whether he'd stolen some lumber for something and was covering it up by telling Ted enough wasn't delivered."

"Oh, that's possible," Jan said, raising her eyebrows, apparently considering the implications of the project coordinator stealing materials. Thoughtfully, she cut another forkful of quiche. "And it could show a pattern of theft from the company."

"It's quite a stretch from embezzlement," Elaine felt obliged to point out.

Jan nodded. "But worth mentioning. What about the other guy? The financial officer."

"Yes, the CFO, Mitch." Elaine pursed her mouth. "Yes, I've thought about that. It's entirely possible. But he's out of the office a lot. And what I can't figure out is why he would do it. His wife's family is wealthy, and by all accounts, it's spread around. They just built a whopper of a house. Who embezzles for the fun of it?"

"That's a valid point."

"Also, and probably more importantly, he was the one who got the information about the donor with the missing tax receipt and realized they hadn't received it. He raised the problem to the authorities. If he had embezzled money, why would he bring it up at all? Wouldn't he want it to stay hidden so he could continue to embezzle?"

"Also a valid point."

After cleaning up the kitchen, the cousins headed upstairs to the sitting room. Elaine glanced surreptitiously at the clock.

Brody hadn't mentioned a time. Oh, she hoped it wouldn't be too late. She wasn't sure her nerves could take it.

"What's wrong with you?" Jan asked. "You seem...edgy."

"Brody and Sasha are coming by, remember?"

"Oh!" Jan's face lit up.

The ringing of the doorbell interrupted her, and Elaine bounced to her feet as if she wore springs. "Let's both get it."

In the foyer, Elaine hit the light switch as Jan went to open the front door.

"Surprise," Sasha said with a big smile as she stepped inside with Brody right behind her. "We just wanted to come by and show you"—she held out her left hand dramatically—"this!"

"Congratulations!" Elaine and Jan spoke simultaneously.

Elaine threw her arms around her daughter and hugged her tightly. "Oh, honey, I'm so happy for you."

"And for yourself," Sasha said, grinning, "since we plan to settle here in town."

"That too." Elaine agreed, moving to hug Brody as Jan embraced Sasha. "Welcome to the family," she said.

Then she took Sasha's hand and examined the ring. The central stone was a gorgeous cushion-cut diamond set in an encircling halo of small diamond chips. Additional diamonds extended partway down the band. It was a dazzling sight.

"Oh my," Jan said. "That is stunning."

"Beautiful choice," Elaine told Brody. "It's a lovely ring."

Brody smiled. "Flawless. Just like this girl."

"How did you ask her?" Jan demanded. "We want details."

Sasha laughed. "We went to the range to practice. He had a backup box of my ammo in his pocket. When I needed to reload, he set the box beside me. I started to pick it up and realized how light it felt. I told him I thought it was empty—" She stopped and looked at Brody.

"And I said, 'I don't think so,'" Brody said, his voice deep as his eyes twinkled.

"Then I realized everyone in the place had stopped shooting, and they were all looking our way." Sasha sniffed, recalling their special moment. "And then he got down on one knee, removed the ring from the box, and asked me to marry him." Her face shining, she looked up at her new fiancé, who dropped his head and touched his lips to hers tenderly.

Jan sighed.

Elaine clasped her hands together. "How perfect. Perfect for you, that is." She chuckled. "Your daddy would be very pleased with your choice of husband, I feel certain."

A tear spilled down Sasha's cheek. "I think so too."

Mother and daughter shared another heartfelt hug. It would be difficult not to have Ben beside her on the day their baby girl married, Elaine realized, but that was a feeling for another day. Today was a day for joy.

"Come on back to the kitchen," she said. "This calls for a celebration."

SALLY'S CAR WAS in its customary space on Friday morning when Elaine pulled into the HMH lot, so Elaine decided to stop in the first-floor office and invite Sally to the Harvest Home Festival next Saturday. It was the only thing she could think of to finagle another conversation with the woman.

"Good morning." Sally sent her a dazzling smile as Elaine pushed through the glass door into the slick, modern office of the brokerage.

"Good morning."

"What brings you this way?" Sally already had powered up her computer, but she removed her hands from the keyboard and leaned back, looking ready for a chat.

"I wanted to invite you to the Chickadee Lake Harvest Home Festival, if you're not already planning on attending," Elaine said. "It's a week from tomorrow. My cousin's on the steering committee, and she'll be there most of the day, though I won't get there till late afternoon."

"Oh, thanks. I've always intended to go to that someday," Sally said, "but I've never gotten around to it. Cassie Markham told me the quilt she's going to be helping you make at the tearoom will be auctioned off at the festival."

Elaine nodded. "I saw the quilt blocks last night, all laid out in the pattern for the top. The woman who's overseeing the project is going to sew the quilt top together, and then next Wednesday we quilt." She smiled. "Well, some of us quilt, and some of us watch."

"Oh, come on," Sally said, "surely you're going to throw a few stitches in there, just for bragging rights."

Elaine laughed. "My cousin Jan will probably insist on it."

"I may run over to Tea for Two on my lunch break next Wednesday and see this work of art in process. Cassie's enormously excited about being a part of it."

"It was my cousin's idea," Elaine said, "and I have to confess I think it's pretty brilliant. I hope it sells well at the festival."

A large oil painting on the wall behind Sally's head caught Elaine's attention. "That's a lovely painting," she said. Remembering the woman's love of Italy, she asked, "Is that the Mediterranean?"

"It is." Sally turned to regard the lovely scene, of a stone balcony crowded with flowering plants overlooking red-roofed villas in the foreground and the blue jewel-toned waters of the Mediterranean Sea in the background. "I have a whole collection at home, and I rotate them every few months. On my last trip, I bought a gorgeous scene of the Venetian canals."

Now Elaine noticed a number of other mementos strewn around the office that looked to her well-traveled eye as if they had come from Italy: a hand-painted ceramic vase, a leather desk blotter and pen cup, and a pretty box with hand-painted paper in it. Sally herself wore an elegant pair of snakeskin pumps that Elaine would bet were of Italian make as well.

Following her glance, Sally tilted her foot to one side to show Elaine the elegant sweep of the shoe. "I buy a pair of shoes every time I go to Italy," she said. "It's a sickness."

Elaine laughed. "Do you travel there often?"

Sally shook her head. "Not as often as I'd like. My last trip was a couple of years ago. You said you lived there for two years, right?"

Elaine nodded. "That was a long time ago."

"Where was your husband stationed?"

"Camp Darby," Elaine told her. "That's in Livorno, on the—"

"Oh, on the western coast of Tuscany," Sally interrupted. "A port city on the Ligurian Sea, right? I've been there. It's certainly a much more modern city than much of Italy can boast of. I hope you managed to get out and see some of the quaint medieval towns in the region."

Elaine nodded. "We always tried to do a lot of touring wherever we lived, to see as much as we could of the different faces of a country and culture."

Sally sighed. "Oh, I can't wait to go back again. I just adore Italy."

"It's lovely," Elaine agreed. "We enjoyed our time there." She shifted toward the door. "I'd better get upstairs. I hope you'll be able to join us at Tea for Two next Wednesday. We're very excited about our first quilting bee."

"*Hmm.* It sounds as if it may not be the last." Sally grinned.

"That's possible, if all goes well," Elaine said, smiling back before taking her leave.

As she exited the brokerage and stepped into the entryway, the front door opened and Mitch stepped in, scuffing his leather loafers on the rug inside the entry to remove any debris. "Good morning, Elaine," he said, his smile warm.

"Good morning," she returned.

"Penny's so grateful for your help," he told her. "She says the promotional project is coming along far faster than she ever dreamed since you've devoted yourself to it."

"I'm glad to be of assistance. HMH is an extraordinary organization. It's a privilege to volunteer here."

"It's a privilege to work here too," Mitch replied as they started up the stairs. "I have a meeting this morning with a new family we're designing a home for. The father's a soldier who lost an arm and a leg in Afghanistan."

Elaine swallowed the lump that rose in her throat at the idea of the young man whose life had changed so suddenly. "How wonderful that HMH is here to help them."

"It is," he agreed. "I don't often get to handle the initial meetings—that used to be Alex's job—so I'm kind of excited about it." His smile dimmed as he turned and held the door at the top of the stairs for her. "Not that I wouldn't be happier if he was still here to do it."

"It's difficult, any way you look at it, right now," she said quietly. "I know all of you are feeling off balance."

"Off balance," Mitch repeated. "What a good description."

Impulsively, Elaine proffered the same invitation to the festival that she'd just extended to Sally.

"I've never attended the Harvest Home Festival," he said, "but I've heard it's great. I bet my kids would enjoy it."

Elaine nodded. "I'm sure they'd be fascinated by some of the exhibitions. And the food can't be beat."

"Sounds like fun," Mitch said. "Maybe we'll see you there."

"Good morning," Ted said as they walked through the main office to the door that led to the staff hallway.

"Good morning," both Elaine and Mitch replied.

Ted handed Mitch a message. "Phone call from the Thurber family," he said.

"Thanks." Mitch was reading the note as he headed down the hall to his office.

"You missed the police," Ted said, catching Mitch as he turned away.

"Oh yeah?"

"Two troopers came here to question us again yesterday. I imagine they'll be in touch with you, since you missed them."

"Okay. Thanks for letting me know. If they come by again, feel free to give them my cell number so that they can track me down. I'll be out of the office in about half an hour for the rest of the day."

As Ted turned back to face her, Elaine noticed a glint in his tie. Was that a diamond? "Your tie tack is lovely," she said. "Is it an heirloom?"

Ted looked down, fingering the object in question with obvious pleasure. "No. Are you into antique jewelry?"

"Not to any great depth," Elaine said. "I just thought it was pretty. My boyfriend deals in antiques and goes to a lot of estate sales, so he would probably know more about it."

"It's an antique filigree art deco piece," Ted said. "I actually got it at an estate sale."

And the diamond in the middle had to be close to a carat, Elaine felt sure. "You have good taste," she said, smiling.

Ted beamed. "Thank you."

"My daughter got engaged last night," Elaine confided.

"Oh my goodness." Ted laid a palm to his heart. "Congratulations. That's so thrilling."

"Thank you."

"Have they set a date yet?"

"Not yet," Elaine said. "I can hardly wait to begin the planning."

"Oh, that's the best part!" Ted looked genuinely excited for her.

"She's my only daughter," Elaine told him, "so I'm looking forward to spending time together as we go through the process." She shifted her weight. "Well, I'd better get moving."

"Oh, wait." He picked up a sheaf of papers from his desk. "I forgot to give these to Mitch. Would you hand them off since you're going that way?"

"Sure thing." Elaine took the papers. She passed Penny's office and walked to the end of the hall. Mitch was on the phone, and when he saw her in his doorway, he beckoned her in and held up one finger, then swiveled his chair and continued his conversation.

Elaine stood awkwardly in front of the desk for a moment. All she needed to do was lay the paperwork down; she didn't need to chat. But Mitch had seemed to indicate that she should wait. As she bent to place the papers on his desk, she saw another single sheet that looked like a chart of some kind. It appeared to be a list of names, followed by sums of money. About a third of the names were checked off. One name leaped out at her: Jean Briggs. That was Mitch's wife's relative whose report that she hadn't received a letter for her donation had triggered the embezzlement investigation. The name didn't have a checkmark beside it. She wondered what that meant, but she couldn't think of a way to ask nonchalantly.

Elaine glanced up as Mitch swiveled his chair back around. "Sounds good," he said politely into the receiver. "Thank you. Good-bye."

"Ted asked me to bring you these papers," Elaine said after he'd hung up.

"Thanks," Mitch smiled and gestured to the stack on his desk. "More donor lists to call through. I have some reassuring to do, as you can imagine. Listen, I hate to trouble you, but would you mind sending Ted back in here for a moment?"

"No problem," Elaine said with a smile.

Penny breezed into the building just as Elaine had sent Ted back into Mitch's office, hung up her jacket, and powered up the laptop she'd been using. "Good morning. You're making me look bad," she said with a smile. "You've beaten me here again."

Elaine laughed. "Shall I arrive at ten after every day?"

Penny grinned. "Far be it from me to make you late. You've been so productive I'd be crazy to want you here even ten minutes less." Penny pulled a yellow pad from her briefcase and tossed it to Elaine. "I reviewed our progress last night. It looks as if in one more week, we'll be there. Thanks to you." She beamed at Elaine.

The day went quickly. The two women were able to finish identifying the dates on the outstanding photos before noon. It was a great feeling of accomplishment to know they would be moving on to the next stage of the project soon.

"Mitch told me this morning that he's meeting with a new family today," Elaine commented. "He said he's kind of excited, since he doesn't usually get to do that."

"That was Alex's job," Penny said absently, moving her mouse with her eyes on her monitor. "I imagine Mitch is pretty frantic trying to keep up with his own work and take on Alex's responsibilities as well. One of the hallmarks of HMH is our personal attention to clients, so there are a lot of meetings on his plate."

"I guess when he reported that missing donation, he wasn't thinking that Alex could have had anything to do with it."

"Oh, I'm sure he didn't," Penny said. "He was as shocked as the rest of us when the police found the checks in Alex's desk. Initially, we all assumed it was just some kind of clerical error. Or at least, I did. I shouldn't speak for the others."

"It's hard to imagine Ted making a mistake of that magnitude, isn't it?"

"There's certainly no distracting him when he's in the middle of The Great Mail Sort," Penny agreed. "I've offered to help him. I thought it would be a good idea to have a backup person recording the donations, just to avoid the exact situation we have found ourselves in with this embezzling they claim Alex did. But Ted says he has a system, and he doesn't want anyone interfering. And he says once the checks go to Mitch, that's his backup."

"I wish I could see him do it again," Elaine said.

Penny laughed. "Any day at eleven, I'm sure you can." She obviously thought Elaine simply wanted another look for the entertainment value. "Although we do have security tapes, if you're running out of excuses to be in the office."

"Security tapes?" Elaine echoed.

CHAPTER THIRTEEN

A surge of adrenaline quickened Elaine's pulse at Penny's mention of security tapes.

"No one ever looks at them," Penny went on. "They're just stored in a drawer in the storage room every two weeks or so when the security guy comes and changes out the disk."

For the rest of the day, Elaine's feet itched to carry her down to the storage room where the filing cabinets were. But it was at the far end of the hallway from Penny's office, and unless she intended to go outside, she had absolutely no reason to enter there.

Then, sometime after three, providence lent a hand. "All right," Penny said. "Since we've pulled all the photos we want to scan, there's no need to keep all these boxes out. Why don't we put them back in storage? Once the scanning is finished, we'll just slip the photos back into their chronological spots, now that we have everything so nicely labeled."

"Great idea," Elaine said enthusiastically. "That will free up some space."

She saved the work on her borrowed laptop, stood, and stretched, and then picked up a box. She followed Penny down the hall, then waited while Penny opened the door of the storage room. She placed the box where Penny directed before they started back for another load. Elaine's mind was racing: how to sneak a peek into the file cabinets to find those security disks?

As she followed Penny from the little room, Elaine glanced at the labels on the pull-out drawers of the three large filing cabinets lined up against one side of the space. A placard on the middle one, second drawer down, read *Security Tapes and Surveillance Information.*

Bingo! Now if only she could swing some way to get a few minutes alone to see if she could find the last month's tapes. For a moment, her conscience pricked her. Would it be considered stealing? It didn't feel like theft, she decided. Just...covert borrowing, perhaps, since she fully intended to return the disks after she and Jan—and possibly Dan—had an opportunity to review them.

No one would miss them, she felt certain. Penny had said nobody ever looked at them, and it certainly didn't sound as if the police intended to pursue a thorough investigation into anyone else when they had Alex right in front of them. And it wasn't just idle curiosity. The more information they had, the better chance she and Jan had of getting to the truth of this embezzlement.

She and Penny carried two more loads of boxes back to the storage room. As they picked up the last group, Elaine managed to leave one box behind. "I'll come back for that one," she said, indicating the single box that did not fit into her arms.

"Thanks," Penny said, juggling. "I don't think I can manage it either."

Elaine felt butterflies rise to tickle her tummy as she returned for the final box and made the solo trek back to the storage room. Thankfully, the door was on a pneumatic hinge that slowly closed after someone entered and released the door. Quickly, she slid the box into place and turned to the drawer she had noted. Once she pulled it open, she was relieved to see that the file with the present year's disks was right in the front. She slipped out the disk for the first half of October, encased in a flimsy plastic cover, and secreted it in the capacious pocket of her skirt.

After closing the drawer quietly, she pulled open the door and stepped out into the hallway—and almost ran into Mitch, who had just walked out of his office.

"Yikes," he said. "Sorry! I wasn't expecting anyone to be in there. What are you doing?"

"Just replacing the last of those photo boxes," Elaine said brightly.

Mitch tapped the briefcase he held. "Forgot some files. Just ran by to grab them. So, the project with Penny is going well, I gather?"

"We're making great progress. Penny says we should finish in another week."

"Great." He grinned. "Since I'm the one who's going to have to give those presentations—at least until they hire a new CEO or Alex is allowed to come back—I'm delighted to hear you're making progress."

"Do you think Alex might return?" she asked, feigning innocence.

Mitch shrugged. "I honestly don't know. But I guess there's always a chance, and I liked working with Alex, so I'm going to be positive until I hear definitely that he isn't."

"That's a good way to look at it." She nodded.

"Elaine?" Ted popped his head through the door of the main office at the other end of the hallway. "Do you have a couple of minutes?"

She smiled. "Sure. Just let me tell Penny where I am."

In a moment, she walked into the office where Ted was behind his desk. He beckoned her around to his side, where he had pulled up a chair for her at his computer.

"I thought you might like to see some of my other pieces, since you liked the tie tack," he said.

"Your other pieces?" she echoed.

He grinned, looking far more approachable than usual. "I have a small estate-jewelry business on eBay. Sometimes I buy online, but often I'll place bids at local sales or make offers on pieces when people contact me through my business website or my Facebook page."

Elaine was shocked. An estate-jewelry business. Her mind raced. This could potentially remove Ted from suspicion since it answered her questions about the expensive jewelry he wore. Conversely, it also could give him a strong motive for embezzling—did he need money to make his purchases? Surely starting up an estate-jewelry business couldn't be cheap.

Unaware of her thoughts, Ted continued. "I got this gorgeous tie tack from a customer referral. I need to sell it, but I'm going to enjoy wearing it a time or two first. Look at this."

He clicked to open a picture in his browser of a lovely woman's onyx cocktail ring with double sets of small diamonds on each side. "This is both dainty and elegant, isn't it?"

"It is lovely," Elaine agreed. "Is that one of yours?"

He nodded. "I just got it last week. Here's another ring I got from the same seller." He opened another window to show her a beautifully faceted cornflower-blue square sapphire on a band sparkling with diamond accents.

"Whoever owned these had wonderful taste in rings," Elaine said sincerely. "That's absolutely beautiful."

"I know." Ted nodded. "And I got them for a very reasonable price." He clicked through several more photos, describing the pieces for her as he went. A Burma ruby and diamond bracelet... emerald drop earrings... less costly stones such as aquamarines, canary topaz, watermelon tourmaline, and fiery opals set in a variety of pieces... Ted had an eye for the unique and tasteful, in a range of prices for many buyers, she noted.

"Oh my," she breathed, leaning forward. The necklace was exquisite: a long necklace of graduated black pearls, with the largest in the center, separated by tiny, sparkling diamonds. "That's stunning."

"I just bought that last week," Ted said proudly.

"You have a fabulous eye for 'must-have' jewelry," Elaine said, smiling. "If I had more disposable income, I'd be buying."

"Wouldn't we all?" Ted asked ruefully. "Fortunately, there seem to be plenty of people out there a lot richer than I."

And again, Elaine wondered if she was wrong about her suspicions. Perhaps Ted wasn't the person she was seeking. But if he wasn't, who was?

Just then, R.J. came striding through the door into the office.

"Hey, you two," he said. "Loafing?" But his eyes twinkled, and Elaine could see he was teasing.

"Taking a momentary break," Ted said with great dignity, all traces of the enthused young man who'd been speaking with her hidden.

Why, she wondered, was Ted less personable with R.J.? Was it simply that their personalities didn't mesh without a CEO around to keep things running smoothly, or was there something more? She found the older man friendly and open.

To that end, she smiled at R.J. and preceded him to the door. "I'd better get back to work," she said over her shoulder to Ted. "Thank you for showing me your jewelry."

Ted was typing again, and he barely looked up. "My pleasure," he murmured.

"Jewelry?" R.J. asked.

"Ted sells estate jewelry online," Elaine told him.

"*Hmm.* My thirty-fifth wedding anniversary is coming up. Maybe I should talk to him about something special for my wife."

"He could probably help," Elaine agreed, thinking that perhaps that would be a good way to loosen Ted's reserve. "R.J., do you ever do any work on the side? I know someone who might be looking for a person to add on a deck to their home." Which, technically, was true. She had overheard fellow congregants discussing that very topic last Sunday, although her opinion had not been solicited.

R.J. scratched his head. "I could recommend a couple of guys who do that kind of thing, but I don't. The last deck I did was nine years ago for my own house." He shook his head, grinning ruefully. "Honestly, after riding herd on construction projects all day, the last thing I want to do when I get home is another one."

Elaine smiled. "Just thought I'd ask."

"My granddaughter's birthday was last week," R.J. went on. "The wife wanted me to build a playhouse, but I knew I couldn't do it in time. We ended up buying one from a local nonprofit that sells them to make money for childhood cancer research."

"So, if R.J. is telling the truth," Elaine said to Jan at home after dinner as they relaxed in the upstairs sitting room, "then he would have no reason to have stolen that lumber, which I thought could be tied to the embezzlement somehow."

After she'd arrived home and told Jan about the security disk, Jan had suggested they invite Dan over to view it that evening. They were waiting for him to arrive.

"That's not necessarily true," Jan said. "Just because he isn't building things doesn't mean he didn't steal the lumber. He could have resold it. And if he did that because he needed money, then we can't eliminate him from possibly being our embezzler. But as far as lumber theft being tied to embezzling, I'm thinking not, since they're such different types of crimes. Also, it seems to me that if R.J. is the embezzler and hoped to pin it on Alex, it wouldn't make sense for him to lift the lumber if he's trying to stay off the radar."

"True," Elaine admitted.

"Did you learn anything else potentially useful or interesting today?" Jan asked.

Elaine laughed, although she wasn't amused. "Did I ever." She went on to share what she'd learned about Ted's online estate jewelry business.

"What?" Jan's eyebrows flew to her hairline. "Good estate jewelry? That could rocket him right to the top of our list of suspects."

"It could indeed. I've been wondering how on earth he pays for his mother's care in a nursing home. I mean, it's not out of the realm of possibility that she had extremely good savings and insurance, but you and I both know how costly it can be to keep someone in a nursing home for any length of time."

Jan nodded. "I feel like he would be worried about money."

"But not if he's successfully buying and selling good estate pieces," Elaine said. "I mean, some of the things he showed me were far, far out of my price range. If he acquired them at any kind of reasonable price, he could be turning a tidy profit. Certainly he could be making enough to pay for his mother's care."

"Which would actually demote him from Suspect Number One," Jan said. "Is that what you're saying?"

"Half of me is," Elaine admitted. "The other half has to think that embezzling would be the easiest way to get his hands on a lot of money quickly."

"If he didn't get caught," Jan said soberly. "Does he strike you as someone who might have framed Alex to avoid his own arrest?"

Elaine shook her head. "None of them strike me that way, to be honest. It's not like anyone's holding a sign that reads, 'I'm a rotten person at the core.'"

"How inconsiderate of them. Our job would be so much easier that way."

As the cousins chuckled, the front doorbell rang.

"That'll be Dan," Jan said. "I'll let him in if you want to get that disk ready."

Elaine quickly turned on the television and set up her computer so she could display the security disk on the TV screen remotely. She rose as she heard Jan and Dan coming along the hallway from the stair landing.

"Hey, Elaine." Dan was dressed informally, in sneakers, jeans, and a red-and-black plaid flannel shirt layered over a black waffle-knit. Over it all, he wore a black fleece zipper jacket.

"Dan, there's a Sale Pending sign in front of Mrs. Battie's house," Jan said. "You don't know who's buying it, do you?"

Dan shook his head. "I hadn't even noticed the change from the For Sale sign."

"It went up Thursday," Jan said. "I'm dying to know who's buying it."

Elaine grinned. "Not us," she said. "Hi, Dan."

"Hi, Elaine." His eyes were dancing. "I hear you pilfered a security disk from HMH."

"I prefer to think of it as borrowing," she said loftily. "I do intend to put it back, you know."

Dan's moment of levity faded. "I know, and I appreciate you taking such a risk." He exhaled heavily. "I feel very conflicted about this. I sent you in there, and you could get in big trouble if anyone ever figured out what you did."

"Well, it was my decision," Elaine said. "You didn't ask me to...borrow a security tape."

"I know."

"Have you talked to Alex?" Jan asked. "How's he doing?"

Dan's face fell even further. "He was formally charged with embezzlement today. So he's not doing too well."

CHAPTER FOURTEEN

Jan winced at Dan's statement. She indicated the blue plush-covered armchair. "Have a seat."

"Would you like something to drink?" Elaine asked.

"No, thanks." Dan shook his head, shucking out of the fleece. "I won't stay long. I just wanted to hear how your first couple of days went at HMH. I've had to force myself not to bug you for daily updates."

Taking her seat again, Elaine curled her legs beneath her. Beginning with the staff introductions, she recounted her experiences.

He listened intently, voicing little opinion.

"I do have a question for you," she said. "Did you know a check was found in Alex's car?"

Dan looked thunderstruck. "What? No." His eyes narrowed immediately.

Elaine had a moment's longing for a chance to use her own fingerprint kit. Unfortunately, since this was an official police matter, there would be no chance of that.

Dan clearly was deeply disturbed by the idea that another check had been found in a different location. If he was that upset about it, Elaine thought, he was really going to be nonplussed—to say the least—when he found out it was a company check Alex had written to himself. She still wanted to wait to share that piece of information until the next time she spoke with Alex and Dan together. It could be helpful to see both men's reactions.

"Alex's little boy is adorable," she said, changing the subject abruptly. "His mother said he was born twelve weeks early."

Dan nodded. "He was in the hospital for a long time. Alex didn't even get to hold him until he was over three weeks old. He was in one of those special incubators, and they had to reach through the portals to change his diaper and stuff." He shuddered. "I never saw him while he was that tiny, but they posted a lot of pictures on social media. Alex's wedding ring fit over his upper arm. I can't even imagine having a child that tiny and fragile."

"Thank heaven for medical advancements nowadays," Jan said. "My younger daughter is expecting her third, and it's comforting to know that even if something doesn't go quite the way it should, there's help available that wasn't even an idea when my kids were born."

"I sincerely hope Amy doesn't have any complications," Elaine said with a shudder. "I can't even imagine the cost associated with a weeks-long hospital stay for a premature baby."

"Insurance picks up a lot of it," Dan told her. "But even so, you could still wind up paying a significant amount because of deductibles and out-of-pocket expenses. I think Alex and

Christa said Miles's total hospital bill was close to three hundred grand."

"Three hundred thousand dollars?" Jan sounded truly horrified. "That's impossible for the average family."

"Insurance paid most of it," Dan assured her. "I think they wound up owing only about $15,000."

"Only? Even $15,000 is a lot for a family to be faced with," Elaine said. She tried as hard as she could to speak in a neutral tone, but something must have given her thoughts away.

"Hey, wait," Dan said sharply. "I didn't mean—I think they have most of it paid off now. Alex would never have embezzled money to pay off personal bills."

"I never said that he had," Elaine pointed out.

"But you're wondering about it now." Dan looked utterly upset with himself. "I just gave you a motive, didn't I?"

"Only if Alex was guilty," Jan pointed out. "The whole reason you asked us to look into this is because you're certain he's innocent."

"And I still am," Dan said firmly. "I'm absolutely positive that he never would commit a crime. Well, maybe a parking violation, but not stealing money from his own company."

"And Alex himself agreed to your suggestion to let us investigate this," Elaine pointed out.

That seemed to settle Dan's ruffled feathers somewhat. "Yeah, and why would he do that if he was guilty?"

"If we learn anything from this disk," Jan said, smoothing over the tense moment, "we can't just take the information to the cops, can we? We'll have to figure out some other way to expose the embezzler."

Dan nodded. "That's it in a nutshell." After a beat of silence, he indicated the TV. "Let's see what's on this security disk."

They all took seats and Elaine started the disk from the beginning. It was the first day of the month. The disk had no sound, so there was no way to know what anyone was saying. Alex, Ted, Penny, R.J., and Mitch walked in and out of the frames. Ted worked at his desk. At one point, Alex brought three people through, introduced them to Ted, and took them on back toward his office.

Elaine explained the layout of the office to the other two, noting that anyone who wanted to go into the back offices or the conference room had to walk through Ted's office first. "I imagine Alex is having a meeting with those folks," she said.

When the time-stamp showed that it was 11 a.m., Ted left the office through the front door. He was back a moment later with the mail, and Dan and Jan got to see firsthand the ritual Elaine had observed.

Ted set the mail on his desk. First, he sorted it by size. Then he picked it up, squared the corners carefully, retrieved his ledger, letter opener, and pen, turned his back, and set all the items precisely on the credenza. From the angle of the security camera, they were prevented from seeing exactly what was going on then.

"What's he doing?" Dan asked.

"Sorting the mail into piles," Elaine said. "I'm not positive what the piles signify, but I think one must be junk mail and catalogs, one is probably donations, one invoices, and so on. I don't know what else there might be."

"Applications?" Jan asked. "Would people who want HMH's help have to send things in?"

"Possibly," Elaine said, "although I think the initial application is online. But I imagine they require a lot of items of information, so there might be things coming in the mail that pertain to applications."

"Bank statements?" Dan suggested. "Or legal matters? That might all go into the pile with invoices, since those things probably would go to Mitch or Alex."

Elaine nodded.

Ted continued to work once all the mail was sorted.

"He slits open the envelopes and makes notes in the ledger," Elaine told the others. "Once that's done, he puts two of the stacks together and takes them to Mitch. At least, that's what he told me. I imagine donations and invoices go to Mitch."

"But Ted is the first one to get his hands on them," Jan said. "That's got to mean something."

They continued watching. Ted left the office, but he was back in seconds. There was only one stack of mail remaining. After entering the information from the ledger into his computer, he replaced the ledger, letter opener, and pen in his desk, and then pulled out a paper shredder from beneath the desk. Catalogs went into a cardboard box which looked to be about half full, and everything in an envelope went through the shredder.

"Junk mail," said Jan. "He's recycling. Good for them."

His mail routine apparently complete, Ted dusted off his hands, then turned to a cupboard and pulled out a spray bottle and a roll of paper towels. He proceeded to clean every surface in the office, including the doorknobs, the light switches, his own cell phone, the office phone, and the pens in the holder on his desk.

"He looks like something of a germaphobe," Jan commented. "Then again, I've read some of those studies about the number of disgusting bacteria found on coins and hands and phones, so I really can't blame him."

Dan and the cousins watched the remainder of the day on fast-forward. At the end, Elaine hit the pause button. "Reactions?"

"Let's find the sections where he opens the mail each day and just watch those," Dan said. "You think that's the most likely way the money is being embezzled, you said?"

"I think it has to be," Elaine said. "Ted lists all the donations in that ledger you saw before recording them in the computer. And then he takes the donations to Mitch, and I imagine he also records them. There would be no way for anyone to steal the checks unless it was done *before* they were logged in. If there ever was a question, Mitch could simply go to Ted and double-check his records against the ledger. I'm not really sure why Ted doesn't just enter the records directly into the computer from the beginning. It seems a little outdated to me to be using a ledger for that purpose."

"Maybe the ledger is just a backup for Mitch," Jan suggested. "I'm sure Mitch uses software to track donations, expenses, salaries, tax, and all that sort of business stuff."

"Probably," Elaine said. "I saw a donor list on his desk that looked like it came from an Excel spreadsheet or something similar, so that would make sense." She moved through the tape to the next day's mail episode, and once again they watched Ted going through his routine.

"It's like that movie *Groundhog Day*," Dan said after the fourth day in which Ted performed practically the same motions over and over.

Jan laughed. "It is."

"But I know there are variations," Elaine said. Her comment was justified over the next several dates, as they saw first Mitch, then Alex, and finally Sally from downstairs deliver the mail to Ted on different days.

After they watched Sally depart from the office, Dan shook his head. "How many people did you say have access to that mail table?"

CHAPTER FIFTEEN

"Theoretically, anyone who walks through the building's front door could pick up the mail if they arrive at the right time," Elaine admitted. "But for embezzling purposes, it would have to be someone who knew that certain donors mail money in at certain times of the month. I tend to discount Penny, because she's always in her office before the mail comes, and she doesn't leave again until lunchtime. R.J. isn't shown on here, and I honestly don't know how much he would know about the donors, but I've left him on the list. Same for Mitch. He's almost never in the office at eleven, so I don't know how he'd manage it."

"Still possible though?" asked Dan.

"Definitely. But I'm just not sure. He's very wealthy. What's the motive?"

"I see. Would the woman from downstairs know anything about donations?" Dan asked.

The cousins explained what they had theorized about the public nature of the nonprofit, and how anyone closely monitoring the website and news articles about HMH might be able to find out who some of the major donors were.

"Also," Elaine said, "I saw a program from a charity auction they held last year, and donors were listed in giving brackets inside it."

"So, it's possible she was able to figure out some of the recurring donors," Dan conceded.

Elaine nodded. "We've tried to consider everything."

"Because the only other two people who appear to routinely be bringing in the mail are Ted and Alex," Jan said.

"Alex didn't do it," Dan said firmly. "So Ted is our strongest suspect. These tapes give me hope that you'll figure out a way to expose him if he really did do it." He checked his watch. "I have to get home. But let me know if you find anything unusual in the rest of the daily watching. And thank you both for everything you're doing to help Alex."

Jan saw him out. When she came back upstairs, Elaine had cued the DVD to the following day's mail routine.

Jan flopped into her chair. "He totally didn't acknowledge that Alex could be a prime suspect. Do you think we should take Alex off the list of potential suspects?"

Elaine shook her head, feeling conflicted. "There's no proof, other than Dan's belief in Alex's integrity, that would make me dismiss him from being a suspect yet. I wish I could, but I don't think we can remove Alex from the list. If anything, these tapes make it more likely that he's our man."

"That's exactly what I thought," Jan said glumly.

ELAINE OPENED THE front door on Saturday morning and waved at Rue, Macy, and Katelyn Conrad, who worked part-time at the

Bookworm. The three were talking animatedly as they walked toward the tearoom. "Good morning, ladies," said Elaine.

"Good morning," Rue said. "We've missed you this week. She's helping out Penny Jillette over at Homes for Maine's Heroes," she said to Katelyn.

"I've missed all of you too." Elaine fingered the edge of the cabbage rose apron she'd donned this morning, one of her favorites. "She mentioned a project she wanted to accomplish, and I volunteered to help."

"Storytime," Katelyn said, apropos of nothing. Then she clarified her statement. "I know the wife of the CFO of HMH, Bettina Dacourt-Vallerand. We have an exceptional story time at the Bookworm and she brings her children every week. And anyway, she's lovely."

"Mitch seems like a very nice man," Elaine said. She was surprised by Katelyn's statement, since Macy had said the Ackerlys were indeed "loaded." "Money isn't everything."

"How's Jan doing with the Harvest Home Festival planning?" Rue asked. "I went to visit Hester yesterday. She's still in the hospital, but they expect to release her today or tomorrow."

"That must have been a terrible fall," Elaine said.

"I'm glad she's improving. Jan seems to have things under control in her absence."

Although she wasn't really sure because she'd been so preoccupied with the HMH embezzlement, Elaine nodded. "Yes, I believe so, except for the corn maze."

"I talked to her about that," Rue said. "Did she get in touch with Mr. Vermeyer?"

Elaine nodded again. "Come on in and she can tell you about it."

In the tearoom entry hall, the three women hung up their autumn jackets and headed into the east parlor, where Rue and Macy often preferred to sit.

Jan greeted them all.

Before Rue could put her question about the Boy Scout leader to Jan, Jan said, "Have any of you heard who's buying the Battie house?"

Rue shook her head, as did Katelyn. "No."

Expectantly, Jan turned to Macy. "Do you?"

"No." Macy shook her head too. "I just saw the sign this morning."

"It only went up recently," Jan reported. "Be sure to let us know if you hear anything."

Rue cleared her throat. "So, I want to know about the corn maze. What was up with Mr. Vermeyer giving you the runaround?"

Jan shrugged. "I don't think it was a runaround so much as he was simply putting off admitting it wasn't going well." She made a face. "Turns out he's short a few volunteers because he had fewer Eagle Scouts than normal. And he stuck his head in the sand and just hoped it would fix itself, I believe."

"Just like a man," Macy commented.

"I know women who do that sort of thing too," Katelyn protested.

"Whatever the reason," Jan said, "I need to come up with at least half a dozen volunteers to help get the corn maze completed next Thursday night."

"I thought you had a committee member who would find volunteers if you needed them," Elaine said.

Jan smiled. "I do, but it's such short notice that I hate to bother her."

"Put Ned and me on your list," Rue said promptly.

"Wish I could," Macy said, "but I've already got plans."

"Frank and I could help," Katelyn said.

"I bet Bob and Nathan would help, and I will too," Elaine said. "We should ask them and maybe Brody and Sasha too. That would make nine of us even if you're tied up with other things, and that should be plenty, right?"

"Right." Jan looked relieved. "Wow, thanks, everyone. I hate to wish my life away, but I sure will be glad when this festival is over."

A familiar face caught Elaine's eye as a new group of customers entered the east parlor. "Sally," she said, "welcome to Tea for Two. I didn't realize you were coming in today." She turned to Jan, who wasn't far behind her. "Jan, this is Sally Murray, who works in the brokerage downstairs from HMH."

Sally extended a hand and shook Jan's. "Nice to meet you. This place is lovely."

"Thank you," Jan said. "We worked hard on it. Choose a table and we'll hope you like the food as much as you do the décor."

"I realized I wouldn't be able to get away on Wednesday to see your quilting bee," Sally said to Elaine, "so I thought I'd stop in today."

"And we appreciate it," Elaine said, smiling. "Take any seat you like." Turning to Jan, she pointed to Macy's group. "I'm going to get their order started."

"I'll take this bunch," Jan said. She glanced toward the door, where several more groups of patrons were arriving. "Looks like it's going to be a busy morning."

Macy and Rue both chose Jan's cinnamon-pecan baklava while Katelyn moaned with delight upon hearing that Rose had made a lemon-cream cheese crescent ring. Macy hesitated a moment after Katelyn placed her order. "I really want to change what I asked for, but the baklava sounds terrific too. And bring a few of those ginger chews."

"Change your order," Rue urged her, "and we'll split them both."

Happy with that decision, all the women also ordered the day's "special-tea," a vanilla chai, and Elaine hurried off to the kitchen to make it. She placed a tray on the counter and swiftly began to assemble teacups and individual teapots, while Rose cut the pastries and slipped them onto plates.

Jan joined them a moment later before busying herself setting up her own tray for Sally's group's order. "Your friend is fond of Italy," she told Elaine.

Elaine laughed. "That's one way to put it. It's practically her only topic of conversation. Apparently, she's traveled there several times. She has Italian décor all around her office and probably her home, she wears Italian-made shoes and jewelry and jackets, she carries Italian-made handbags, and heaven only knows what else."

"She's wearing a Murano-glass-and-platinum necklace," Jan said helpfully, and Elaine laughed.

"Of course."

"She says she's planning a two-week vacation to Florence, where she has family, in the spring."

"Wow," Elaine murmured. "She told me her last trip there was two years ago. That's a lot of travel to Italy, even if she stays with family when she's there."

"And a lot of Italian mementos," Jan added. "Italian leather isn't cheap, nor was that necklace she's wearing."

"She has a painting in the office she mentioned switching out for another from her home." The cousins looked at each other.

"Maybe," Jan said, "we should look a little more closely at how much Sally knows about donations to HMH."

The fall harvest was traditionally celebrated that weekend in October at Lancaster Community Church. Parishioners were invited to bring their home-canned goods as well as freshly harvested fruits and vegetables, all of which were donated to a local food pantry after the service.

It was one of Elaine's favorite services of the year. Shocks of corn stood tall at the sides of the altar, and pumpkins and gourds flanked the steps at the front of the sanctuary. People streamed forward at the pastor's invitation to place their gifts on the altar: glistening jars of fruit preserves, pints of pinto and green beans, tasty-looking canned dill pickles, peaches and pickled beets, a bushel of ripe red apples and much more.

Among those approaching the altar were Brody and Sasha. Both carried baskets from which they removed half a dozen jars of canned tomatoes. Elaine smiled, knowing the couple had helped Brody's mother, Abigail, can them just a few weeks earlier. She was filled with a powerful mixture of gratitude, pride, and pleasure. Having her daughter living close enough to visit with was a joy, one she did not take for granted after Sasha had been so far away for several years. And they were going to be planning a wedding soon! She could hardly wait to get started.

Pastor Mike's sermon was powerful, likening one's actions as the planting of a seed and the tending of a garden. When he spoke of bringing out the good in someone as a harvest and of harvesting a smile, Elaine couldn't help but think of Ted Harrington, whose demeanor had warmed significantly as she took the time to get to know him. Ted, she had to admit, had by far the most opportunity to embezzle from Homes for Maine's Heroes. She was going to be sad and disappointed if she uncovered evidence that pointed to the young man who was so good to his mother.

After church, Elaine and Nathan were filing out of the sanctuary right behind Bob, Jan, Brody, and Sasha when Jan said, "Hey, I almost forgot to ask all four of you if you're free on Thursday evening. It turns out I need folks to help set up the corn maze for the Harvest Home Festival. Any volunteers?"

"I'm in," Bob said. "What does this involve?"

"Some carpentry, some muscle, and I'm not exactly sure what all else," Jan confessed. "The Boy Scout leader planned it, but he's short on help."

"I'll help too," Nathan said. "I assume you'll be there?" he asked Elaine, who nodded.

Sasha glanced at Brody. "We can come too. But we'll need directions, since neither of us has ever been to the festival before."

"Wonderful. Thank you all. I'll e-mail you directions tomorrow," Jan promised.

As they started for the parking lot, Elaine spotted Dan and his family. Leaning forward, she said to Jan, "I think we should ask Dan if he and Alex would have time to drop by this afternoon. I'd like to talk with Alex again."

Jan stopped and turned around. "You think we need to ask him about that check that was found in his car, don't you? The one he wrote to himself that he neglected to mention to us or to Dan?"

Elaine nodded. "There's something weird about that, don't you think?"

Jan nodded. "It makes me wonder what else he's covering up."

They approached Dan and set three o'clock for a meeting before heading back to Elaine's car for the short trip home.

As they pulled out of the lot, Elaine said, "I want to stop at the store and pick up a bridal magazine."

Jan chuckled. "Oh, what fun! Maybe we can get a couple. Even if Sasha's in no hurry to look at them, it's never too early to start looking for a dress for you." She waved to some of their fellow congregants. "It was a nice service today," she began. "I—wha-!"

An enormous thud shook the car, and it suddenly listed to one side. There was a shriek of something that sounded metallic as the car's momentum carried it forward a few feet.

CHAPTER SIXTEEN

Elaine turned off the car and unclipped her seat belt. "Are you okay?" she asked Jan.

"Yes." Jan unfastened hers as well.

From outside the car they could hear urgent, excited voices, and a moment later both doors were pulled open, and people assisted them from the car.

"What happened?" Elaine looked at her car, oddly angled with the back passenger corner low to the ground.

"Your right back wheel fell off," Dan said. He'd been about to pull out of the church lot but had parked and run over to them.

"Fell off?" Elaine was bewildered. "Just fell off?"

Dan shrugged. "Sometimes the lug nuts become loose. As you drive, they get looser and looser and suddenly—*bam*." He clapped his hands together sharply. "It's a good thing you weren't going at any significant speed," he said. "I've seen this happen on the interstate, and people have been badly injured." He squatted and looked at the tire lying at the side of the road where it had rolled after it fell off.

"Have you had your tires rotated recently?" he asked. "Or had anything done that would have meant this tire was removed and put back on?"

Elaine shook her head. "No. In fact, it's due for inspection in two months."

"Hey, Dan?" Russell Edmonds, another churchgoer who was the marine postman for the area, approached.

Dan and Elaine both turned to look at him, alerted by the tone in his voice. "What's up?" Dan asked.

Russell opened his closed fist to show small metal pieces. "Lug nuts and covers. They were in a little pile in the grass behind where she parked."

Elaine blinked. "What?"

Jan sucked in a dismayed breath. "Someone took them off on purpose," she said in a stunned voice. "Right?"

"That's what it looks like." Dan's voice was grim.

"But why?" Jan asked. "They had to know we wouldn't get very far without them."

"Thankfully, we didn't." Elaine swallowed.

"That's pretty brazen," Russell said, his brows drawn together. "Someone did this right here in broad daylight during church. That's a pretty rotten prank to play."

Dan stood and scanned the area. "I have to call this in," he said.

ELAINE'S CAR WAS towed to a nearby garage, because the troopers who responded wanted to fingerprint her hubcap. They promised to get it to the garage by tomorrow.

The general consensus was that it was probably a prankster playing a really bad joke, and that it could have happened to anyone in the congregation.

"You can borrow my car," Jan assured her over lunch. "I doubt I'll need it."

"Thanks." Elaine was inconvenienced, but both cousins felt very thankful there hadn't been serious damage or injury.

As the cousins left the kitchen and headed upstairs, a piece of paper on the floor beneath the coat hooks near the back door caught Elaine's eye. She stooped to pick it up, righted it, and read it.

The hairs on the back of her neck rose. "Jan."

Her cousin was ahead of her. "What?" Turning, she saw Elaine's face and immediately came to her side. "Oh my," she said softly. "This must have been in the car."

"I bet it was on my seat," Elaine said. "It must have gotten stuck to my coat."

Together they stared at the little note.

Next time, it will be worse.

Jan read the computer-printed words aloud again, then said, "We'd better call Dan, Elaine. This note means—"

Elaine held up a hand, trying to stay calm. "Let's hold off on speculation until Dan gets here."

Jan's face was troubled, but she nodded. "All right."

DAN ARRIVED AT two thirty, although Alex wasn't joining them until three.

He did a very satisfying double-take when Elaine handed him the note she'd found and placed in a plastic bag. "This changes everything about what you're doing at HMH," he said ominously.

"Well," she said, "I don't know. Maybe this note has nothing to do with the embezzlement or HMH."

"I think you should report it," Dan said, concern rippling his forehead.

"I'm not ready to do that yet," Elaine replied.

Just then, the doorbell rang, signaling Alex's arrival and curtailing the conversation, much to Elaine's relief. They moved downstairs into the smaller west parlor. Elaine had brewed coffee, suspecting the men would prefer that to tea.

"Hello," she said, pulling open the front door to admit Alex. "Come on in."

"Hi," Alex said, a warm smile on his face. "I'm looking forward to hearing how the investigation is going."

Elaine led them to the table just as Jan returned from the kitchen with a tray laden with several different pastries they had left over from the Saturday trade.

"Oh man," Dan said. "I'm going to have to go to the gym and work off the calories I'm about to pick up, aren't I?" By unspoken agreement, Elaine knew they wouldn't be sharing the morning's unsettling events with Alex.

Elaine chuckled. "Possibly. Tea or coffee?"

Both men looked relieved as they asked for coffee.

"Not that I don't like tea," Dan said. "But I'm more of a coffee kind of guy." He picked up one of the cinnamon baklava from yesterday. "This looks fantastic."

"It is." Alex was a mouthful ahead of him. "Amazing."

Jan brought the drinks in sturdy mugs rather than the more elegant teacups they used for the business.

"So, here's where we are," Elaine said. She reviewed what she had learned.

"Wow," Alex said when she'd finished. "I must walk around with my head in the clouds. I had no idea Ted's mother was in a nursing home, or that Sally loves Italy, but I did know Mitch has little kids. He talks about them all the time."

"You probably had a lot less time than I do to make small talk," Elaine said. "Mitch has been running around like a crazy man trying to keep all the balls in the air."

"I bet." Alex looked unhappy. "No way can one person handle both the CEO and CFO work for long. I wish this had never happened. I wish we could get it straightened out so I could get back to work."

"I know." Jan cleared her throat. "Alex, we have a couple of questions for you."

"Shoot," he said immediately, setting down the slice of lemon cream-cheese crescent ring he was already halfway through, having polished off the baklava in record time.

Dan sat up straighter. His law enforcement instincts were sharp, Elaine realized. He sensed something was coming that he wasn't going to like.

"We know the troopers investigating found checks hidden in your office and another in your car," she said. "Are those the only places you know of?"

Alex nodded, his gaze becoming watchful.

Elaine took a deep breath. "I'm sorry if you find this offensive, but I have to ask: at any time have you ever borrowed money from Homes for Maine's Heroes?"

"Now wait just a minute—"

Alex held up a hand to silence Dan's protest. "It's all right," he said. He sighed. "I already told the police about this, and I'm sorry I didn't tell you. All of you. I guess I was hoping this would be resolved without it ever coming up."

"Without *what* coming up?" Dan growled.

Alex took a deep breath. "I don't think the police believed me, but this is the truth." To the cousins, he said, "Our son was born six months ago at twenty-eight weeks gestation, twelve weeks before his due date. As you can imagine, he required a lot of medical intervention, and that resulted in an enormous hospital bill. We had good insurance, but we still had a sizable deductible. Also, there were things that weren't covered. The bottom line was that when all the insurance paid out and was settled, we still owed a lot of money."

Elaine nodded. Thanks to Dan, she and Jan were aware of that already.

"We began planning to pay it off, but the hospital wasn't very helpful. They wanted us to pay a lot more per month than we felt we were able to. I was really afraid they were going to turn us over to collections, which would ruin our credit rating. One day, Mr. Burgess, the president of the board, asked me how things were going, and it was one of those bad days when I had just gotten off the phone with the hospital billing department, and I just spilled it all."

He stopped and rubbed his eyes. "He offered to let me borrow the full amount through HMH and repay it out of my paychecks at whatever amount we felt we could handle."

"When was this?" Jan asked.

"First thing in the morning, the same day the cops came," Alex told her.

"And how much was the check written for?"

Alex looked down. "Fifteen grand."

Dan's jaw looked like a chunk of granite, hard and unyielding.

Alex picked up the story again. "It was done on a handshake and no papers were drawn up. Mr. Burgess was in a hurry because he was leaving right away to go out of the country and he said I should go ahead and write the check immediately, and draw up a repayment schedule when I had a chance. He watched me write it, and I promised to pay it back over a twelve-month period with interest, which I felt we could manage."

Jan said, "So then a little later the cops found the check in your car made out to you in your own handwriting—and no documentation to back up your story."

Alex nodded. He looked defeated. In a quiet voice, he said, "Mr. Burgess was already gone and I didn't want to ruin his vacation."

"And now Mr. Burgess has had a stroke." Elaine had a sinking feeling in her stomach. "And there's no way to prove what you've said."

"I can't prove it right away," Alex stressed. "I hope when Mr. Burgess recovers, he can tell them it's true."

"He had a stroke," Dan said in an angry, exasperated tone. "He may never recover enough to speak on your behalf." He clearly was stunned, and Elaine couldn't blame him. Alex hadn't shared this information with him. It must have been a major blow.

"Was your car locked?" Jan asked. "Was there any way someone else might have known that check was in your car?"

"I've never seen the need to lock it." Alex shrugged helplessly. "Guess that's going to change now. And I didn't tell anyone, so I doubt anyone knew it."

"No wonder the unit thinks you're guilty." Dan clutched his head in his hands. "Do you realize how bad this looks?"

Alex nodded at Dan, his face sober as he assessed his friend's evident anguish. "I'm sorry I didn't tell you. I guess I always believed that an innocent person would be exonerated once the truth was told."

"But they have no way of being sure you told the truth," Dan said. "No evidence to back you up, remember?"

Intervening before Dan could heap more recriminations on his friend's head, Elaine said, "We obtained the security disk for the first couple of weeks of October, and we've been reviewing it. It seems to us that someone with access to your mail must be pulling the donor checks before they can be logged into your system."

"That makes sense." Alex nodded. "In fact, that makes a lot of sense, because I think Mitch would have caught it sooner if they were tampering with his accounting."

"Is that even possible?" Elaine asked. "Wouldn't all those things be password-protected?"

Alex nodded. "Yes, but they're shared files. Mitch and I both have access, as does the board treasurer. The president too, come to think of it. I'd have to check to see if that's all."

His temporary lift of spirits seemed to desert him. "But I can't check anymore." He heaved a sigh. "On the mail stuff, pretty much all of us and Sally downstairs have access to that mail before it comes into the office. So how can you figure it out?"

"If someone's taking envelopes out of the mail before it reaches the office, we're going to have to think of how to address that," Jan said. "But we're hoping to get some clues from the security disks."

Hope shone in Alex's eyes. "Have you looked at the disks yet? Maybe they'll show something helpful."

If Alex was guilty, wouldn't he be perturbed or worried that they were going to such lengths to find out the truth? Perhaps he simply was sure there was nothing incriminating on the disks.

Or perhaps he truly was innocent. Elaine couldn't decide. Her gut instinct told her Alex was being truthful. But this case was far too important for her to take anything on faith. They needed facts. Hard, cold, incontrovertible facts that either exonerated Alex DeRone—or proved his guilt.

"We haven't found anything yet," she told him. "But we're still looking."

After a few more minutes of stilted conversation, Dan and Alex rose to leave.

"Thank you for the coffee and pastries," Alex said, "and for everything you're doing on my behalf. As much as I hate the thought, I'm afraid one of my coworkers must have stolen those checks. And I guess that means I've been framed."

Dan's lips were pressed into a tight, hard line. Elaine could tell he wasn't happy with his friend. As Alex preceded him out the door, Dan lingered a moment.

"Just be cautious this week, okay?"

After Elaine promised, and after they'd closed the door behind the two men, Jan said, "So the president of the HMH board has had a massive stroke, and since the cops won't be able to confirm Alex's story about the borrowed money that led to the check he wrote himself, they probably think he's lying."

"In a nutshell," Elaine agreed. "And the worst part is, I can totally understand why the cops didn't believe him when he tried to tell them Mr. Burgess encouraged him to write that check. If I told you the board president, who just happens to be incapacitated, gave me permission to borrow $15,000 and write myself a check, with absolutely no paperwork to prove my story, mightn't you find it pretty suspicious?"

"I would," Jan agreed, "if I were a cop. I think the difference for us is one of perspective. The troopers' investigation is trying to prove Alex *is* guilty, while we are trying to prove he's *not*. You and I are more inclined to want to at least believe his story could be true than the police would. And it also means you and I are more willing to look at other suspects."

"True," Elaine said slowly. "The police are focusing mostly on Alex. I haven't seen a single sign that leads me to believe they're even considering anyone else at the company."

"Because they have a suspect who looks pretty good for the crime," Jan said.

"And while I want to be open-minded, I think we need to be very careful not to assume he's innocent just because

Dan believes in him." Elaine hated to say it, but she felt she had to consider that maybe Alex was gaming them all, even Dan.

AFTER ELAINE LEFT for HMH on Monday, Jan and Archie were finishing the morning setup when Camille Lapole came by the tearoom.

"I have the quilt top stitched together," Camille announced. "I wanted you to see it just in case you wanted to rethink the placement of any of the squares."

Jan gaped at her friend. "Camille. You have sewn this together. I would never tell you to rip out your work and mess with the placement at this point. Besides, we agreed on the final layout last week, and I thought it looked terrific. I'm sure it looks even more amazing now."

"I think it looks pretty good," Camille agreed. "I just want you to be happy with the final product."

"Let's look at it," Jan said. "*Hmm*. I don't think the dining room table is big enough. How about in here?" She gestured to the west parlor.

They pushed a couple of tables together and unfolded the quilt top, displaying it fully.

"Oh my," Jan breathed. "Camille, it's even more gorgeous than I remembered. I can't wait to see it quilted!"

"I brought along a couple of ideas for that," Camille told her. She held up a round metal ring to which she'd attached half a dozen different plastic quilting templates. "Around the border, I was thinking we could use this leaf chain. Wouldn't that be a nice accent on the ivory?"

"It would," Jan agreed. "I love the autumn theme."

"Me too. I found a couple of other templates that would also work. Here in the corner blocks, I thought we might use this pumpkin with vine. We could repeat the leaf motifs in the internal borders and use either the pumpkin or this sunflower in each block of the background fabric. Then for each of the designed blocks, just do a border inside the design all around the edges."

"That sounds wonderful!" Jan couldn't contain her enthusiasm. She waved a sheet of paper on which she'd noted everything they would need and began to dig things out of the bag she'd set on a chair. "I know some people will bring their own thimbles, but I got extras. And hand-quilting needles. Here are two fabric markers for the templates, and large safety pins. What have I forgotten? Oh, thread." She dug around in the bag. "That's weird. I bought a bunch of that good twenty-eight-count cotton thread. But I don't see it in here."

"We can't really use regular thread," Camille cautioned. "That's forty- or fifty-count; not nearly strong enough for quilting."

"I know." Jan was flustered. "I am positive I purchased the good stuff. I guess if I can't find it, I'll buy more before the quilting bee starts on Wednesday."

Elaine did not have the chance to observe Ted's mail routine on Monday. But shortly after two, Penny said, "Elaine, I need two hundred stamps for these letters I worked on over the weekend, but I need to proof the letter and set up the mailing list to select the recipients. Would you mind terribly running to the post office for me?"

"Of course not." Elaine rose and grabbed her coat. "I may walk if it's as nice as yesterday."

"No problem." Penny dug in her desk and withdrew a credit card, which she extended to Elaine. "Put the expense on this card, and I'll add it to my monthly report when you get back."

"Thanks." Elaine placed the company credit card in her wallet, then replaced it in her handbag and slipped into her jacket before leaving. Ted and Mitch were both in the front office when she came through.

"Hey, Elaine," Mitch said.

He had two dark gray bank bags in one hand, which he passed to Ted. "These need to be deposited today."

Curious about where Ted would take those bags, Elaine thought fast. "I'm headed for the post office," she said, trying to act casual. "Want to walk with me as far as the bank?"

"Sounds good. Give me a minute."

The post office and a cluster of three bank branches were in the same direction along Camden Avenue.

"Did you tell R.J. to talk to me about a jewelry purchase?" Ted asked as they walked along.

Elaine nodded. "I hope that was all right."

Ted grinned. "It was more than all right. I talked him into purchases for his wife and a couple of Christmas gifts for other relatives. Thanks."

Elaine laughed. "I bet his wallet is still wincing."

"They were really nice pieces," Ted said. "The recipients will be thrilled."

Ted turned off before she did and entered a local branch of a state bank. "Don't wait for me," he said. "This might take a while."

Why would it take a while to make a couple of deposits? Elaine nodded, but she couldn't think of a viable reason to argue, so she walked on toward the post office and purchased her stamps. Ted had avoided her eyes when he'd told her not to wait. Was she being overly suspicious, or had there been something a little off about his desire to avoid her?

What could it hurt, she reasoned, to see if he was up to something? If he wasn't, she would be happy to feel foolish. She watched the bank from a lobby window inside the post office. Sure enough, it wasn't long before her patience was rewarded. Ted exited a moment later. He did not turn back the way he had come but walked in her direction.

Elaine quickly shrank back into a far corner of the post office, hoping it was not Ted's next stop. But as she watched from the edge of a window, he marched right on past and down the street, continuing away from the office.

Cautiously, Elaine exited the post office again. Ted appeared to be oblivious to other pedestrians around him, and he barely paused at the walk light at the next corner, so she followed him from as great a distance as she could while still keeping him in sight. He continued for another block, and then to her surprise, he crossed the street and entered a second bank.

Her pulse raced. Could this be the bank with the dummy HMH account? Maybe he'd already deposited the bank bags at the previous bank, and simply had a personal account at one of these other banks. Was it possible that Ted had just taken the opportunity of the errand to attend to personal business? Or had he set up a fake HMH account?

She didn't want to believe it was possible, but she was pretty certain that someone with technical skills and a lot of ingenuity, someone "trustworthy" and with a certain amount of authority, stood a decent chance of figuring out some way to steal from an employer. She supposed it was a good thing most people were decent and honest, or surely there would be even more trouble with embezzlement and corporate theft than there was.

She didn't want Ted to see her here, she realized, or he might suspect she'd been following him. Quickly, she turned and hurried back to Homes for Maine's Heroes.

In the office, she hung up her things and handed Penny the requested stamps and the credit card. "Here you go," Elaine said. "Two hundred stamps."

"Thank you so much," Penny said. "I've got the mail-merge working right, finally, on these letters, so I should be able to get them out by the end of the day. You go ahead and keep working on that PowerPoint."

Elaine returned to the computer she had closed before leaving the office. "I saw Ted going to the bank," she said casually, "but I couldn't catch up with him." She hoped Penny didn't realize that this was a fishing expedition, plain and simple.

"Oh, he does that every afternoon," Penny said. "Alex told him he could just put things in the safe and go every second or third day, but you know Ted. It's part of his routine, and his routines are practically unshakeable."

Elaine smiled. "That's probably a good trait in an office manager. Not much seems to go wrong on his watch."

Penny snorted. "Just embezzlement."

Elaine was surprised. Penny was usually kind and even-tempered. "Do you think Ted had something to do with that?"

"I don't know." Penny sighed. "I'm not privy to much of the financial stuff. I review publicity campaigns with Mitch to see how well certain things did. We check the percentage of donations per items sent out for mail campaigns, and with other things like radio and television, we have formulas to try to measure how effective they are. But I don't deal with donations directly like Mitch does, so I really can't say whether Ted did it. I just think he has a lot of opportunity, and Alex doesn't."

"So, you don't think Alex did it?"

"I don't know." Penny looked distressed. "I only know he's a really good guy to work for, and he's brought this company a long way since he came onboard. I've worked here for five years, and that yahoo who was here before Alex didn't care one bit about helping veterans. Or anyone, really, other than himself."

Interesting to hear her research corroborated, Elaine thought, but how to steer Penny back to Ted? "The police seem fairly sure Alex did it."

"I know," Penny said, "but it doesn't make sense to me."

"What bank does the company use?"

"Northeast Harbor. Why?"

"Just curious. Ted did go into Northeast Harbor but then he went on down the street to Waterville S&L."

Penny shrugged. "Maybe he has his own accounts there."

"That's what I figured." Although it wasn't the only answer she had.

TUESDAY FOUND ELAINE fidgety and wishing she hadn't offered to devote quite so much time to the HMH project. She hadn't spoken to Sasha alone since the young couple had come by to share the news of their engagement, and Elaine was eager for a mother-daughter chat. Sasha was never prone to vocalizing any dreams about her future wedding, so Elaine had no clue about what appealed to her. Would she want a large wedding or small? A simple dress or something elaborate? Elaine was betting on small, simple, and elegant rather than ostentatious, but she'd wait and see what her daughter said.

True, she wanted badly to help Dan figure out who really was responsible for the embezzling attempt, but in addition to thoughts of wedding planning, today she desperately wanted to be back at Tea for Two, helping Jan, Archie, and Rose prepare for their first-ever quilting bee tomorrow.

Finally, she gathered her things, more than ready to leave. "Don't forget I can't be here tomorrow," she said to Penny. "But I'll see you first thing Thursday morning."

"Oh, good luck with the quilting bee and your Autumn Tea," Penny said. "I wish I wasn't working. I don't really have enough time at lunch to come over, enjoy myself, and get back, but it sounds like it's going to be such fun."

"We hope everyone will think that," Elaine said.

She left the office and hurried down the stairs. But as she hit the last tread, she heard someone say, "Hi, Elaine!" Sally was locking the door of the brokerage office. Under her arm was a dark-gray bank bag that looked exactly like the ones Ted had been carrying earlier.

CHAPTER SEVENTEEN

Elaine tried hard to get a glimpse of the logo on the bag Sally was carrying to see which bank it was from, but the bag was flipped the wrong way and partially hidden by Sally's jacket sleeve.

"Or should I say, 'Bye, Elaine'? It's been so nice seeing a fresh face around here. How much longer will you be helping Penny?" Sally appeared unaware of Elaine's distraction.

"I really don't know," Elaine said. "Until our project is finished, I suppose." *Or until I figure out who really tried to steal those checks.* She couldn't think of a way to bring up Sally's bank bag without sounding false or suspicious. Was it a personal deposit or the brokerage one? If there was any way to find out, it was beyond her mental capabilities at the moment.

Finally back home, Elaine walked into the tearoom through the garage door. The kitchen appeared to be shut down for the day. On the large work island, cups, saucers, and teapots stood ready for the upcoming day's business and several large platters were stacked as well.

"Hello?" she called. True, it was 4:15, so Rose and Archie could be gone, but where was Jan?

"Up here!" her cousin's voice called.

Elaine doffed her coat and set her handbag down before climbing to the second floor.

Jan was in her little craft room. "I'm losing my mind," she announced.

Elaine's eyebrows rose. "This is probably not the best time for that, given tomorrow's schedule."

"Ha." Jan snorted. "Have you seen a small bag with spools of heavy-duty quilting thread in it? I can't find it anywhere, and we need it for tomorrow."

Elaine shook her head. "No, but I'll help you look. Did you ask Rose and Archie?"

Jan nodded. "Yes. No luck there."

Elaine searched the sitting room, even checking beneath the cushions of the couch and chairs, in the wastebasket, and in other unlikely places. No thread.

"It wouldn't be downstairs," she mused as she trudged back to report her lack of success to Jan.

"No," Jan said. "I always bring anything like that up here into our private space if it's not something we need for the business."

"But this sort of is," Elaine pointed out.

"Well, I suppose so," Jan said, "but what I meant was I normally would only keep something downstairs if it was for my baking needs or for serving our customers. Most everything else, like our decorative items, for example, is stored up here."

"Gotcha. So where do you think it could be?"

"I have no clue. I've been looking off and on since I realized it was missing when Camille came by to finalize our quilting plans yesterday morning."

"You don't suppose you could have thrown it away by mistake, do you?"

Jan shook her head. "I wouldn't have done that, and Rose and Archie swear they didn't. I guess I'm headed for the fabric store. If I wind up finding the first bag, I can always return it or save it for next year's bee."

"Now that's what I call planning ahead." Elaine chuckled. "I'll get dinner started while you're gone."

"Oh." Jan stopped as she was about to descend the steps. "I almost forgot. Sasha called. She wanted to know what time Amy's appointment is tomorrow. She's going to drop by for the big reveal. I also told Tara and Paula, and they're both going to try to make it too."

Elaine smiled. "That's great." It was such a thrill having her daughter close enough to drop by on occasion. She still hadn't gotten used to it. And now there was a wedding to plan! She began to hum as she headed to her room to change clothes.

THE SUN ROSE in a cloudless blue sky on Wednesday, heralding a good day for the Autumn Tea. Elaine included thanks for the good weather in her morning devotions before heading downstairs for breakfast.

She found Jan already wrapped in a large white baker's apron, pulling a tray of something delicious-smelling from the oven.

"Good morning. What is that?" Elaine demanded as she sliced a banana bran muffin and placed it in the toaster oven. "It smells like heaven."

"Morning. It's the chocolate pecan pie," Jan reminded her, "and it's fabulous. Rose made one yesterday just to be sure it was perfect. It was better than perfect."

"I can feel the calories piling on just from smelling it." Elaine really wanted coffee, but she didn't want the odor of coffee permeating the tearoom on this day that would feature tea, so she made herself a cup of the special red rooibos tea they would be serving that day. If she was going to serve it, she should be able to describe it from personal experience.

Rose arrived as Elaine was finishing breakfast and immediately went to work on another of their day's specialties.

After cleaning up her breakfast dishes, Elaine headed for the back porch, where they had bags of gourds and miniature pumpkins keeping cool. Earl Grey was sleeping in a shaft of sunlight. She stooped to pet him and he arched and stretched beneath her hand, purring loudly. She carried the bags into the parlors and added them around small pots of chrysanthemums decorated with ribbon that Rose or Archie had placed on the tables late yesterday. The small autumn touches formed the tables' special centerpieces for the day.

Moving on, she went to the linen closet and pulled out the box of folded napkins. She had ordered cloth napkins in gold, burgundy, brown, and orange that added to the festive colors, and she placed them at all the tables and left the rest at the wait station for quick table changes.

"What's next?" she asked Jan when she returned to the kitchen. She felt "out of the loop" after having been away from daily tearoom work so much.

"Camille should be arriving any minute," Jan said, "and she'll need help getting the quilt laid out in the west parlor and ready for the actual quilting to begin. Oh, I almost forgot—there are sunflowers in a vase on the back porch too. Could you put those on the He or She table? I wanted to use potted ones, but I couldn't find anything suitable, so I had to buy some cut ones. We can give them to Amy after the gender reveal this afternoon."

"Nice idea. I'm sure they'll be fine," Elaine reassured her.

Two minutes before ten, Elaine, Jan, and Camille stood around the unfinished quilt.

"I can hardly wait to see it finished," Jan said. "This is going to be gorgeous." It had been sewn together in six rows of five blocks each, with the rosy ivory border fabric between. The autumn motifs in the blocks vied for the viewer's attention.

"You can see how I've laid it out so two sides are rolled up," Camille said. "This morning, we'll work on quilting the long sides, beginning with the blocks and working outward to the border. Ten of the twelve quilters already know how to quilt, so I expect we'll have from the center out to the side edges complete by one o'clock when we switch shifts."

From the foyer, Archie called, "Incoming! I'm unlocking the door," and the day began.

WITHIN MINUTES, THE chairs around the quilt were filled, and quilters were beginning to ply their craft. Rue and Macy were the only two nonquilters in the morning group, and Camille had paired herself with Macy while Hetta Grimm, a chatty, grandmotherly woman whose wedding reception had been held at Tea for Two on Valentine's Day a couple of years ago, mentored Rue.

Macy, Jan observed, was being uncharacteristically quiet as she carefully followed Camille's instructions. Her mouth was set in a determined line, and Jan couldn't help but grin. Macy was good at many things, and she would be good at this by the end of the day, no doubt.

The bee was exactly what Jan had envisioned, and from the delight Elaine radiated, Jan thought her cousin felt the same. Silver needles flashed like minnows in a stream as the women dipped them through the fabric, each quilter finding her rhythm.

Customers coming in for tea placed their orders and then wandered over to observe the quilting. People stopped to read about Amy's baby and place their guesses in the He or She jars.

It was lunchtime before Jan realized it. Rose prepared toasted baguette slices with herbed cream cheese spread as well as what she called "BLGs": bacon, lettuce, and grape with whole-grain bread triangles on wooden skewers. In addition, they had put together "quilt sandwiches" of tuna salad and lettuce between small slices of whole-grain bread. Jan also had made up an autumn fruit salad of apples, pears, and dates combined with walnuts, dried cherries, cinnamon, and honey in small cups, as the second shift of quilters gradually replaced the crafters from the morning session.

"Elaine," Jan said, after meeting one of the new arrivals whom she didn't know, "come over here."

Elaine joined her, an inquiring smile on her face.

"This is Hyacinth Dupree," Jan said. "She tells me you've met her husband, R.J., at Homes for Maine's Heroes. Hyacinth, my cousin Elaine Cook."

"Oh yes," Elaine said, extending a hand. "He mentioned to me that you were coming to quilt. Welcome to Tea for Two."

"Thank you," Hyacinth said. "A friend of mine spoke about this event at our quilting club, and I thought it sounded like a wonderful project to volunteer for."

"We think so," Elaine said. "It's our first time trying it, so if you have any questions, please speak up."

"I'm sure it will go just fine," Hyacinth said comfortingly. "R.J. says you're a worker bee who knows how to get things done."

Elaine laughed. "Well, that's kind of him. He's a pretty hard worker too." Jan could see her cousin was angling to confirm something as she added, "He told me you couldn't talk him into building a playhouse for your grandchildren, so you purchased one from a charitable organization. I think that's great."

"Well," Hyacinth said, "I'm retired, and I have the time to make curtains and rugs and things for the inside, but building the whole thing would have been a ton of work for him. He pointed out that he already spends all day supervising 'builds,' looking at house plans and getting involved in pretty much the entire building process, and he'd rather spend his at-home time with the family. I couldn't blame him. And we were happy to support that nonprofit, so it worked out well in the end."

Jan's thoughts whirled. That was pretty much exactly what R.J. had told Elaine. If R.J. had stolen that lumber or embezzled money or stolen those checks, there had to be another reason entirely.

"Will he retire soon?" Elaine asked.

Hyacinth nodded. "He's thinking maybe one more year."

"Oh boy," Elaine said. "And then what? Might you travel?"

The woman shrugged. "Maybe a little. We're not really the kind of folks who feel the need to traipse all over the globe. We enjoy doing things in the community and spending time with our kids and grandkids."

Jan could see her thoughts were running parallel to Elaine's as Hyacinth took her place at the quilt: another potential motive for money was down the drain. But perhaps the couple didn't have a good retirement nest egg. Elaine had said she liked R.J., and Hyacinth seemed equally pleasant. Jan wished their sleuthing didn't require them to be so suspicious of people who appeared to be perfectly nice, but they had to figure out who stole those checks and how they got in Alex's desk.

If Alex hadn't done it himself, a little voice reminded her.

"But I'm not ready to quit," Macy said, breaking into Jan's thoughts. Elaine was pointing to the clock. The changing of the guard should have been completed around the quilting table.

"I think Macy's hooked on quilting. She hasn't even paused to eat yet," Jan said in an undertone as she came to Elaine's side.

"Maybe someone won't show up and I can stay for the afternoon." But to Macy's obvious chagrin, all of those slated to quilt from one to four arrived, eager to participate.

"We'll do it again," Jan promised her. "I had no idea this would be such a hit."

And a hit it was. As the afternoon wore on, more and more people dropped by. If all the tables were full and they had no chance of being served, they asked if they could just watch the quilters. Soon it was standing room only in a solid ring around those seated at the quilting table.

Jan was almost too busy to think about Amy's ultrasound. But not quite—as the afternoon wore on, she checked the time surreptitiously again and again. The ultrasound had been scheduled for two o'clock in Augusta, so with luck, Van and Amy would be coming sometime around three.

Suddenly, Elaine's hand fell on Jan's shoulder. "There's Sasha, Tara, and Paula," she said. "And Amy and Van are right behind them."

"Hi, everyone." Amy was glowing. "We have news!"

Jan leaped to her feet and rushed to the door to embrace her daughter. "Come right over here," she said. "You're going to make the announcement and then pull a name from the jar that guessed the right gender."

"Wait," Sasha said. "I have to put in my guess." She scribbled her name on a slip of paper and ostentatiously slid it into the She jar.

SASHA SLIPPED TO Elaine's side. "Isn't this great?" Sasha asked. "I hope she gets a girl this time. I'd love to go buy the frilliest pink dress I can find."

Elaine looked at her daughter, surprised. "Have you suddenly turned into the pink frilly type?"

"I might not want to wear it myself," she said with a laugh, "but it sure would be fun to have a little girl to fuss over, wouldn't it?" Sasha grinned and waggled her left hand with its glittering engagement ring under Elaine's nose. "You never know what this could lead to, Mom."

Elaine pressed a hand to her heart. "Nothing would delight me more," she said, surprised to feel her throat grow tight. Impulsively, she said, "I don't want to rush you, honey, but when you're ready to begin planning your wedding, I'd love to invite Brody and Abigail to join us for dinner so we all can chat about it together."

"That's a great idea," Sasha said. "Maybe in two or three weeks? That would give Brody and me a chance to talk about the general direction we'd like to take."

"It's a date!" Elaine said. "Without a date, at the moment." They chuckled together.

"Oh, this is so exciting!" Jan raised her voice. "Anyone have a last-minute guess to place in our gender-reveal contest?"

The tearoom fell silent.

"Amy and Van," Jan said. She indicated the decorated table and the pumpkin. "What will your little seed be?"

CHAPTER EIGHTEEN

Amy and Van glanced conspiratorially at each other, grinning.

They walked to the table. Van picked up the pumpkin Jan had set there, and Amy pulled something from her pocket. Jan couldn't see what it was because the couple huddled over their work.

Then Van turned and held the pumpkin high, and everyone burst into spontaneous clapping and laughter. The stem of the pumpkin sported a polka-dotted pink bow, and they had tacked on lavish black eyelashes and a cupid's bow of red lips where the face should be.

"We're getting a girl!" Amy said above the din. She glanced up at her husband with a look of such love that Jan's throat tightened. Van bent and brushed a kiss across her lips, and everyone clapped again.

Amy blushed, and Jan laughed, stepping forward to embrace her daughter.

"Oh, Mom," Amy said, tearing up, "you're going to get to make tutus and princess costumes!"

"I can't wait to meet our little bundle of pink," Jan said, hugging Amy tightly. In a more normal tone, she indicated the jars full of guesses. "Here," she said. "Now you get to choose the winner of our little gift basket."

Her daughter thrust a hand into the jar decorated with pink. She pulled out a slip of paper, then handed it to Jan, who unfolded it, turned it right side up, and read out, "Candace Huang."

A squeal erupted from the east parlor, where the reporter was seated with several other women. Employed by the *Penzance Courier*, Candace had helped the cousins in the course of their investigations more than once in the past. "Thank you," Candace said as Jan met her halfway across the room to deliver the small basket.

As Jan returned to the foyer, she saw Tara and Paula congratulating Van while Sasha and Amy shared a hug. Blonde hair mingled with brown as the cousins embraced. It warmed Jan's heart. She thought that she might be nearly as happy as Elaine that Sasha had moved to Lancaster a few months ago.

Within the next hour, the afternoon quilting group had finished the borders of the harvest quilt. The tearoom emptied, and Rose and Archie finished bussing the last tables and worked on getting the kitchen gleaming again.

"The quilt looks fantastic, better than I could have hoped if I'd done the entire thing myself," Camille said as the last quilter departed.

"I agree. I want to buy it for myself," Jan said, grinning. The autumn motifs in the border squares and edging formed pleasing patterns, and the squares themselves were now highlighted with stitching that gave them more of a 3-D look and texture.

"I think you'll have a lot of competition," Elaine remarked, coming to stand beside the pair and surveying the quilt. "I heard at least ten people saying they might come to Harvest Home and bid on it."

"Come on, everyone," Sasha said. "Let's get these tables all put back where they belong, so Mom and Jan don't have to do it by themselves after we leave."

With Van, Sasha, Jan, Elaine, Camille, Rose, and Archie all working and Amy supervising, or so she said with a wink, the return to normalcy went quickly.

Later in the evening, the cousins were seated in their favorite spots in the sitting room, catching up on the news and recuperating from the busy day. Elaine and Jan discussed their conversation with Hyacinth Dupree.

"I'm almost ready to count him out. He just doesn't make my antenna quiver," Elaine said, making Jan chuckle. "You know what I mean?"

"I do." Jan sobered. "So, who does?"

Elaine spread her hands. "I suppose Ted is probably the top contender, because I know he's in need of large sums of money. Then again, Sally has to burn through a lot too, with all her Italy trips and the amount of high-quality goods I have seen."

"What about the board members?" Jan asked. "Any way one of them could be involved?"

"I sure don't see how. I really think whoever it is has or had access to the mail, and that the checks they were going to steal never got recorded in the company books. So, it almost has to be one of the staff members or Sally. But I've thought it would be tough for Sally to have hidden those checks in Alex's desk on short notice, and she also would have to have had a way to find out that they had gotten a call from an unhappy donor."

"Maybe she has an accomplice," Jan said. "We haven't considered the possibility that there could be two people involved in this."

Elaine stared at her, appearing dismayed. "You're right. I hadn't even thought of that."

"And that still means Alex could be involved," Jan said glumly.

Elaine felt oddly wary as she entered Homes for Maine's Heroes on Thursday morning. Perhaps it was the letdown after the excitement of the wildly successful quilting bee. Or perhaps it was the knowledge that someone she had met recently was an embezzler.

"Good morning," Ted said. "How did your event go yesterday?"

Elaine smiled. "Very, very well, thank you."

"Wonderful." He opened a desk drawer. "Look what I bought over the weekend. Mid-twentieth century. I just had to share it with someone."

"It" was a stunning bracelet of moonstones and some deep-red stone set in bright-yellow gold in an arty design that alternated heart-shaped leaf and love-knot links.

"Oh, that's gorgeous," Elaine said, reaching for the bracelet and draping it over her wrist. "Are those rubies?" As she admired the bracelet, she noticed that Ted had a deposit slip in front of him. It was not for the business, but for Waterville Savings & Loan, the second bank he had visited on Monday. There were notations for two items, which she couldn't read, but the amounts totaled over $8,400. Not an insignificant sum, Elaine thought, mentally raising her eyebrows.

"Burmese," Ted confirmed. "And there are matching earrings. I have a lady who adores moonstones that I think will be interested."

"If she's not," Elaine predicted, "you'll have no trouble selling this. It's just lovely."

"Mitch's wife buys from me occasionally," Ted said. "If I don't sell them to the moonstone lady, I may show them to her."

"I have a friend that I'd like to surprise," Elaine said on the spur of the moment. "I'd love to find her something pretty and unique, but I'm afraid my budget runs more to the fifty-to-one hundred range than it does to items like this. Do you ever handle cheaper pieces?"

"I handle less expensive pieces," Ted said, "but I am always on the lookout for quality, so I wouldn't call them cheap. Let's see." He tapped his finger against his chin. "I recently bought several pieces of vintage rhodochrosite at an estate sale. Some are set in silver, and others are polished strands of beads. If you'd like to see some things in that price range, I could bring them in tomorrow."

"That would be great," Elaine said. She thought immediately of Amy. She did plan to get the baby a gift, but she had wanted to get Amy something special to commemorate the birth of her baby. What better than a strand of rosy pink beads to celebrate her baby girl?

"How did you get started in this business, Ted?" she asked. Of course, she couldn't ask the question that was really on her mind: where did you get the funds to start buying expensive jewelry?

"My mother's elder sister passed a few years ago," Ted said. "She had a sizable collection of vintage jewelry, and since she had no children, she left it to me. I'm the last of my line, except for a second cousin who's not really into the family connection." He grimaced and then brightened as he continued his tale. "I catalogued it and started learning more about it, sold a few of the pieces that didn't appeal to me, and then bought a few more that did. That was around the time Mother went into the nursing home. I realized I could use Aunt Sophie's collection to help me fund Mother's care, although I've never mentioned it to Mother. She would have been very upset to hear that I'd parted with her sister's things." He hesitated, looking far away for a moment, and then resumed his tale. "But I owe Aunt Sophie a great debt of gratitude for taking that burden off my shoulders. I like to think she knew she was leaving me a nest egg to help care for her baby sister. I don't know what I would have done. It's not like I could keep my mother in a nice facility on my salary." His eyes glistened with tears. "Watching her deteriorate has been terrible, but I sometimes imagine how much worse it could be if she wasn't in a lovely place with caring staff that I trust to watch over her."

"Oh, Ted," Elaine said. "What a sweet story. I'm certain your aunt would be so proud of what you've done with her gift." She handed him the bracelet, patting his hand as she did so. "Your mother is very fortunate to have such a caring son."

As she headed back to Penny's office to begin her day, Ted's words replayed over and over again in her head. She suspected that he had just told her the absolute truth and that he had nothing whatsoever to do with the embezzlement.

As she and Penny were returning from their lunch break later, Mitch came down the hallway toward them. "Hi, ladies," he said. "Where'd you go for lunch?"

"Diego's," Penny said, naming an eatery on the next block. "Best quesadillas on the planet."

Mitch nodded. "Can't argue with that. Wish I could have joined you." He ran a finger around his collar and grimaced. "I lunched with my father-in-law, who is no barrel of laughs, let me tell you."

Elaine thought that was sad. She had loved Ben's parents, both of whom had passed on some years ago. "I'm sorry," she said.

He blew out a deep breath and plastered a smile on his face again. "Eh, that's okay. I'll put up with her father in order to have her as my wife and the mother of my kids, no matter how crazy the little ones make life for us." He playfully rolled his eyes.

"Oh, I remember those times," Elaine told him. "Those were some of the most beautiful but toughest years of my life. Hang in there. It gets better and better."

Mitch smiled. "That's what I've been told."

"What are you doing here anyway?" Penny asked. "I thought you had meetings all day."

"Yeah, one got canceled. Gonna get some work done here before the next meeting." Mitch then headed down the hall, and the two women entered Penny's office.

As Elaine booted up the laptop she had been using, Penny said, "We've plowed through this so fast that I think we'll probably be done by the middle of next week. Even if we're not finished by, say, Wednesday, do you want to plan for that to be your last day?"

"Sure, if you think that will wrap things up," Elaine said. But her mind was racing: now she was on a real deadline to figure out who had stolen those checks and framed Alex.

At home later, she voiced that concern to Jan over dinner. "I think we'd better talk to Dan again. Maybe without Alex this time. We've got to figure out who planted those checks in Alex's office."

"We can't do it tonight. We're due at the Harvest Home maze site at six so we can help set that up. Bob and Nathan are meeting us here in... *eek!* Ten minutes! I've got to get ready. But let me call Dan quickly and see if he can make it tomorrow night."

Jan gave Dan a call while Elaine cleaned up the dishes from the shepherd's pie and peaches they had shared for dinner. "He'll be here at seven," she reported, before she rushed upstairs to brush her teeth.

Bob arrived just a few minutes later, and Nathan pulled in before Elaine could close the door behind him. "Do you want to drive?" she called to him. "If you want to wait a second, we'll come out, and we can ride over there together."

"Sounds good." Nathan stayed in the car while Elaine grabbed her handbag and jacket and called to the other couple to hurry.

"How was your day?" she asked as she slid into the front seat. She leaned toward him for a kiss and then sat back to buckle her seat belt.

"Productive," Nathan said. "I met with a woman selling an entire set of Meissen china and several pieces of furniture that had been in the family for three generations. We came to a mutually agreeable price point."

"Oh, good for you," Elaine said.

"How about you? Exhausted after yesterday?" They had spoken on the phone last night, and Elaine had told him all about the quilting bee, the tea, and Amy's gender reveal.

She grinned. "Not at all. A little excitement is good for the soul. And here we are, about to go put up Jan's corn maze, and the Harvest Home Festival is this weekend. Never a dull moment!"

Jan and Bob came out and climbed into the backseat of Nathan's Cadillac. "Hey there," Jan said. "Thanks for chauffeuring us."

"No problem," Nathan said. "Is the corn maze in the same place it always has been?"

"Yes. Right beside the parking lot near the pavilion," Jan said. The Harvest Home Festival had been held in the same site for as long as any of them could remember. Elaine and Jan had attended it as small girls, giggling and chasing each other through the crowds and stuffing themselves with chicken corn soup, fried pickles, caramel apples, and homemade ice cream.

It was a lovely drive along the edge of the lake to the park just outside Penzance. There was one lone truck in the parking lot when they arrived, and the scoutmaster, Mr. Vermeyer, hurried over, looking distinctly relieved to see them.

Jan introduced him to everyone.

"My Eagle Scout should be here any minute," he told her, "and his father's coming to help."

"We have some other folks coming as well," Jan told him.

"Oh, good." He gestured toward the truck. "I have the lumber and tools here to make the tower, as well as bundles of corn shocks to post at the entrance and bales of straw for underfoot."

Just as he finished speaking, several other vehicles pulled in. Brody and Sasha emerged from his truck. Rue and Ned Maxwell and the Eagle Scout and his dad were right behind them, and as they walked toward the group, Frank and Katelyn Conrad pulled in, waving as they parked.

The men carried in the lumber and bales. As the scoutmaster began to lay out the pieces of the tower and explain the construction process, the Eagle Scout approached Jan, Elaine, Sasha, Rue, and Katelyn. "Mr. Vermeyer and I have been monitoring the growth of the maze throughout the summer and fall, and we've got the various pathways pretty well cleared, but as you spread the straw along the paths, if you see a cornstalk protruding or one growing somewhere that it shouldn't be, tug it out and use straw to help smooth over the spot where it came from."

While the cousins and the others set to work, the scout placed battery-operated lanterns at intervals around the maze, since it was getting hard to see as the twilight gave way to darkness.

The time passed quickly, as did the work with so many people to help. By seven thirty, the tower had been erected in the center of the maze, all of the pathways were firmly layered with straw, and the sign had been pounded into the ground at the start of the maze.

"Thank you all so much for your help." Mr. Vermeyer looked at the group gathered at the entrance to the maze, his face wreathed in smiles. "I thought I might still be here at ten o'clock tonight, trying to finish this myself."

Jan chuckled. "Glad we could help," she said. "Thank you for coming out, everyone. I hope to see you all at Harvest Home on Saturday."

CHAPTER NINETEEN

Friday was possibly the most frustrating day Elaine had experienced yet in her embezzlement investigation. While it was a good day in terms of the amount of progress she and Penny made toward completing the PowerPoints they were working on, Elaine did not learn one single new thing that might help resolve Alex's troubles.

Mitch was out of the office all day. R.J. came in first thing in the morning and then hurried off to a series of meetings, saying he wouldn't be back in until Monday. Ted was there, but Elaine had no opportunity to talk to him. He was on the phone when she arrived, transcribing something wearing headphones when she and Penny went to lunch, and busy the rest of the time. Even Sally had taken a personal day and wasn't working downstairs at the brokerage.

Over lunch, she couldn't resist pulling the bridal magazine she'd bought from her bag and dangling it under Penny's nose. "Want to look through this with me?" she asked.

"I'd love to," Penny said. "This is so exciting."

"It is." And life was a funny thing, Elaine reflected. Whoever could have predicted that she and her daughter would both be in the advanced stages of serious relationships at the same time? And in all likelihood, there would be an engagement in her future too, someday. It was a sweet and tempting thought.

The euphoria faded though when she got home to find Jan waiting to hear about her day. "Nothing happened," she reported glumly. "Not a single thing. After today, I will only have Monday, Tuesday, and Wednesday of next week to figure this out. It could be even less than that if we finish sooner."

"It's a good thing Dan's coming tonight," Jan said. "We can discuss everything you've learned this week and see if he has any new ideas for you to investigate at the office, or if there's anything else we can do."

As she opened the door and invited Dan in at seven, Elaine said, "I hope Charlotte's not too annoyed with you coming over here again. I thought we really needed to review all our information."

"Charlotte's as worried about Alex as I am," Dan said. "If you can help unmask the real criminal, she's all for us meeting. Have you found some new information this week?"

Elaine took him upstairs to the sitting room. "Some. Maybe you'll have some fresh insights."

As they entered the room, Jan turned to greet Dan. "Hello there. Thanks for coming over."

"This looks official," Dan said, smiling as he took in the setup. He took a seat on the couch.

Jan had dragged an easel in from her craft room. A large piece of paper had been clipped to it, and she brandished a marking pen. "I thought it might help us organize our thoughts if we review each suspect and the things we know about them."

Dan's smile widened to a grin. "I feel like I'm in the squad room."

"That might be a good thing," Elaine said.

"Before we start," Dan began, "you haven't received any more threats, right?"

"None," Elaine said. "Nothing else has happened."

"Good," Dan said, sighing with relief.

"Maybe it was a random prank after all," Jan said. "I was worried that it had something to do with this investigation, but that doesn't seem likely, does it?"

It was Dan's turn to shrug. "We can't tell. But I wouldn't stop being careful. Whoever did it knew you wouldn't get very far before that tire fell off, so it could have been a sort of warning shot. Keep your eyes open when you're out in public, and don't go anywhere alone for now."

"We can do that," Elaine assured him. "Now. Let's get started. First, we should list the suspects."

"How many are there?" Jan asked. "I'll make columns."

Elaine counted on her fingers. "Six."

"All right." Jan said. "Shall we start with Penny?" Down the side of the chart, she wrote, "Means, Motive, Opportunity, Notes" each in its own block.

Elaine nodded. "Penny is a suspect because she works in the HMH office."

"But we discounted her," Jan said, "because a) we know her personally and consider her honorable, but more importantly, b) she told Elaine she doesn't have much to do with the donations end of the business, and c) Elaine has seen for herself that Penny does not appear to have much access to the mail or the money. She said herself she's not allowed to touch the mail."

"On the other hand," Elaine said, "if the person who threatened me did so because they figured out that I'm in the office 'under cover,' Penny would make the most sense. I've asked her enough questions that, if she's guilty, she would probably be alarmed at my inquiries. Plus, keep your friends close and your enemies closer..."

"Right. But also there's the question of motive," Jan said, tapping the one empty block beneath Penny's name. "If she needs money or spends beyond her means, we're not aware of it. And to go to such lengths to threaten you, there must be something we're missing if she's the guilty party."

"Well, she did say she and her husband been saving for a new car, and they've almost got enough," Elaine said, "but they're looking at a gently used Honda HR-V, and even the top-of-the-line models are under twenty grand. That doesn't warrant the great sums of money that have been stolen."

"So, she's on the list, but low," Dan summarized.

"Agreed," Elaine said.

In the "Notes" column under Penny's name, Jan wrote, "Low prob—good character, no known motive."

"Alex is next," Jan said.

"He's low for me," Dan said, "for the same reason Penny is for you: I know him personally and consider him honorable."

"But there's a crucial difference from Penny," Jan pointed out. "Penny has little access to the mail. Alex had more. As the CEO, he has been known to come and go at various hours, and Sally told Elaine that sometimes Alex picked up the mail from the downstairs table and took it up to the office. He had opportunity," she added gently. "He also has more to lose, which could mean he's sending Elaine threats."

"But why?" Elaine asked. "If he's telling the truth about the loan sanctioned by Mr. Burgess, he didn't need to steal money in the first place."

"Lots of the embezzlement happened before the board president offered him the loan, though," Jan said.

"True," Elaine admitted.

Dan's eyes had been swiveling back and forth from one cousin to the other as they spoke. "Okay," he said. "So, he had means and opportunity, and possibly motive. I still feel like he's low probability. I just can't believe I would have known him practically my whole life and not realized he's capable of this."

"Fair enough." Jan's gaze met Elaine's across the room. Quietly, she turned and wrote, "low prob—good character," in the notes column.

"Ted Harrington, the office manager, is next. You thought he seemed like the most likely candidate, right?" Dan's voice sounded hopeful, and he sat a little straighter.

"Means," Jan said. "We know he handles all the incoming mail. He logs it in. It would be incredibly easy for him to slip an envelope out of sight without logging it in."

"Especially given that weird routine he has with his back to the security cam," Dan said. "I can't imagine why he'd do that if he didn't have something to hide."

"It could be just part of the way he's always done things," Elaine cautioned. "He's pretty compulsive. The attention to detail is certainly within Ted's character. Which doesn't mean I believe the two things are connected," she tacked on.

"Motive," Jan said. On the board, she wrote, "Mother's care + building small business."

"Yes, although as of yesterday, I'm not so sure," Elaine said. "I had a conversation with Ted in which he explained that his aunt left him a sizable vintage jewelry collection when she passed away several years ago. From what I gather, he's been able to parlay that into a profitable business buying and selling high-quality estate jewelry. He intimated that the business has allowed him to pay for his mother's care."

"Nursing homes are expensive," Dan said. "That would have to be some kind of side business."

Elaine nodded. "I saw a deposit ticket for what could be his personal bank account yesterday for two items totaling well over $8,000. And he showed me a new item he just bought that I suspect retails for at least five grand, if not more."

Dan sat back, nonplussed. "Why's he still working for HMH?"

Elaine grinned. "I know, right? I didn't think to ask him that. But maybe the business doesn't make enough to support him *and* his mother. Or it's possible he simply likes it. The rest of the staff seem to derive a lot of job satisfaction from their roles in helping veterans get customized homes and equipment. Ted may feel the same way. He's a good office manager."

"Any chance that deposit wasn't his personal one?" Dan asked.

Elaine grimaced. "Funny you should ask." She went on to elaborate her suspicions about Ted's visits to the two banks. "But I'm just not sure," she said.

Jan was scribbling on their list of suspects. "All right," she said. "So where do I rank him?"

Elaine considered for a moment. "Before yesterday, he was right at the top of my list. But now... now I'd have to say I'd put him somewhere in the middle of the pack."

"Got it. Let's move on to R.J.," Jan said.

"I guess I'm not sure," Elaine said. "There was that altercation about a missing lumber shipment at one point, and it did occur to me that if he would steal lumber, he might steal money. But that didn't pan out."

Jan was writing as fast as she could. "So low probability?" she asked.

Elaine hesitated. "Yes, for now. Only because I haven't learned anything about him to date that would lead me to believe he's our guy."

Dan studied the board. "All right. So, tell me about this Sally."

"Totally possible that she did it," Elaine said.

Dan sat up straight. "Really?"

"I like her," Elaine said, "so I hate saying that. But she checks most of our boxes. She has access to the mail. She knows exactly when the mailman comes every day. She even carries the HMH mail upstairs on occasion if she's going up there and it's still on the table. She's friends with Penny, so it's possible she has some knowledge of who the big donors are, or she could find that online too. And most importantly, she spends lavish amounts of money on her trips to Italy. I cannot even name all the things she's shown me that she bought on this trip or that, and they weren't inexpensive trinkets either."

"But how," Jan inserted, "would she have known that someone called in about a missing donation?"

"Penny," Dan said.

"Okay, but how would she have hidden the checks in Alex's desk?" Jan turned to Elaine. "Does she come upstairs regularly? Would her presence be unusual?"

"I've never seen her when I was there," Elaine admitted. "But I suppose it's not impossible. R.J. and Mitch, and I imagine Alex, could all have been out of the office at the same time. Ted and Penny never go to lunch at the same time so that there's always someone there, but if Ted wasn't in the front office, Sally might have been able to sneak in and get past Penny." Although that sounded fairly improbable to her, even as she said it.

Dan studied their list as Jan wrote the information beneath Sally's name. "What about Mitch?"

"Well, as CFO, he certainly would be in the best position to know who the regular donors are."

"But he's wealthy," Jan said to Dan. "Indecently so, we've been told. Married to money. And he's the one who was responsible for the theft being reported to the police. So it's totally possible he did it, but why on earth would he need to embezzle if he's wealthy, and why would he alert authorities in the first place?"

"Plus, from what I can tell," Elaine said, "he's a mild-mannered man and a father of two young children. Threatening my safety seems totally out of character."

Jan stood with the marker poised, contemplating the chart they'd generated on the sheet of paper. "What now?"

"I don't know," Elaine said, rubbing her temples. "I feel like my thinking is circular."

"Why don't we look at the security disk again?" Dan suggested.

"Good idea," Jan said. She set the easel aside and used the remote to cue up the disk.

Elaine dropped into a seat and slipped off her shoes, propping her feet on the coffee table, while Jan curled up in an overstuffed chair and Dan stayed where he was on the sofa.

Jan sighed as they started where they'd left off, and they watched Ted go through his mail routine. "Remind me again why we offered to help you with this investigation."

Dan chuckled. "You know that saying about police work being 99 percent boredom and 1 percent terror? I can vouch for that."

The trio sat quietly for the next quarter-hour as they scanned through a week or so of Ted's mail routine.

Elaine cleared her throat. "I'm just not seeing anything. Maybe we should—"

"Wait!" Jan leaped out of her chair, stabbing her finger on the remote to freeze the action on the screen. "Did you see that?"

Dan looked as startled as Elaine. "See what?" He stood and took a step closer to the screen as Jan fumbled with the remote.

Jan backed up the recording. "Watch the date," she said, hitting the play button again.

A moment later, Elaine and Dan both exclaimed as they realized what Jan had caught on to already—there was a date missing.

"Could that have been a day the office was closed?" Dan asked. "It seems to automatically skip weekends. Maybe it was programmed to skip a day on purpose."

Jan thought for a second. "The skipped date was October 10th. That was a Tuesday," she said. "I know because I was the lay reader at church on Sunday the 8th."

Dan looked at Elaine. "Is there any way to find out who was in the office on the day this was deleted?"

Elaine frowned thoughtfully. "I don't know. Unfortunately, I can't tackle that until Monday."

"Why would a day have been deleted?" Jan was pacing back and forth. "The only reason I can think of is that someone didn't want the mail routine to have been observed on that day."

"Or perhaps it wasn't the mail routine, but something else that happened in the office," Elaine said. "The entire day is missing."

CHAPTER TWENTY

"There's absolutely no reason for a day to be missing on that tape unless there was something the record showed that would implicate someone," Jan said. "It's just too coincidental that the missing date would happen to directly precede Alex being charged. On Tuesday, the tenth of October, someone in that office did something that would have looked suspicious to anyone who reviewed that DVD."

They all sat silently for a moment. Then Elaine spoke up. "What if I call Penny?" she suggested. "Let me try to get the information we need without actually telling her we need it."

Dan nodded. "Give it a shot. We have to use some unorthodox methods to figure this out."

Giving one short, sharp nod, Elaine picked up her phone. She scrolled through her address book until she found Penny's entry, then touched the screen to call the other woman.

"Hi, Penny," she said when her friend came on the line with an easy, "Hey, Elaine."

She hit the speaker button so Jan and Dan could hear Penny's responses.

"Something's come up and I may be a little late on Monday morning," Elaine improvised.

Penny chuckled. "You don't have to report to me," she said. "You're a volunteer, remember?"

"I know," Elaine said. "But I wouldn't want you to worry." She forced a laugh. "I hate to ruin my perfect attendance record. Anyone looking at those security tapes could attest to my early-bird habits."

There was a snort from the other end of the phone. "I told you no one ever looks at those. Well, Mitch took a few out recently, but he put them back the next day. That was before you started coming in, anyway. I promise I won't give away your secret. You can keep your early-bird honors."

Elaine laughed, more than a little relieved that Penny had accepted her flimsy conversational gambit *and* given her exactly what she was seeking. "Thanks."

JAN FELT ALMOST breathless with nerves on Saturday morning as she made up a batch of her cinnamon-raisin muffins that were always such a big hit. The Harvest Home Festival officially began at 11 a.m., and Jan was expected to give a little pep talk to the volunteers at 10:30.

Elaine breezed in from the office. "You look pale. Feeling okay?"

"Just nervous. I hope you said a prayer for me this morning. I am so afraid something's going to go wrong today."

"It won't," Elaine predicted confidently. "You had good help and Hester's notes. You've got everything under control. I'm sorry I can't head over earlier, but as soon as the tearoom closes, I promise I'll come."

"It's all right," Jan said, pressing a hand to her stomach to quell the butterflies. "I appreciate you, Rose, and Archie handling the tearoom today."

"As I appreciated you freeing me up to help Dan figure out what really happened at HMH," Elaine told her.

"We decided that together," Jan reminded her. "And look how much you learned from being inside the organization."

"But not enough yet," Elaine said. "I'm going to call the wife of the board president, Mr. Burgess, today and ask if I could speak with him. I thought perhaps he might be well enough now to vouch for Alex having his permission to write that check to himself. It doesn't address the other checks, but it might help to at least convince the investigators it's not such an open-and-shut case."

"Good plan," Jan said.

Rose arrived, and then Archie. Jan vacated the kitchen to rush upstairs and dress in layers for what might be a chilly day outside at the festival. The last she'd checked the weather, it was supposed to be sunny, so she was hoping to be able to shed a few layers at midday, but this was central Maine, so there were no guarantees.

Hefting the tote bag that contained Hester's notebook and files, Jan headed downstairs, grabbed her coat, and walked to the door. "Harvest Home duties call. Thanks to you all for covering for me."

"Good luck," Elaine said. "See you later."

Back in her office, Elaine looked up the home phone number for the board president, Mr. Burgess. She wanted to call early so that she might catch his wife at home before she went to spend the day with her recuperating husband.

After two rings, an older female voice picked up. "Hello?"

"Hello, may I speak to Mrs. Burgess, please?"

"This is she. Who's calling?" The woman sounded abrupt and suspicious. If she got the same number of robocalls the tearoom did, Elaine couldn't blame her.

"My name is Elaine Cook," she said quickly. "I'm a volunteer with Homes for Maine's Heroes, and I was there when Mr. Burgess had his stroke. I'm so sorry that it happened. We were all wondering how he is doing." She really did want to know.

"He's improving," the president's wife told her. "He was moved to a rehab facility yesterday. You people realized what was happening and got help so fast that they think they were able to prevent some of the worst damage. So thank you for that."

"Of course," Elaine replied. "Would there be any time I could visit and speak with Mr. Burgess? There are a few questions that we need—"

"Oh, no, no. I already explained this to Idris Cole, the board vice president. My husband cannot speak well enough to converse yet, and his doctors do not want him upset or agitated in any way. No, I'm afraid that the very earliest you might be able to talk with him about HMH concerns will be after Christmas. In the meantime, I suggest you speak with Mr. Cole. He's dealing with anything my husband was involved in."

"Did he tell the police about the check Alex DeRone wrote himself out of the company funds?" Elaine asked.

"Oh, I know nothing about that," Mrs. Burgess said.

Disappointed, Elaine thanked Mrs. Burgess for her time, and ended the call.

SIX HOURS LATER, the festival was well under way. The judging of the various contests had been completed and blue ribbons decorated the winning entries. Jan had been busy putting out small fires of minor crises all day, but as four o'clock passed, she began to relax. There were still several ongoing exhibitions and events to get through, but the bulk of the work was done. The crowds had grown larger as the day passed. A folk band composed of mandolin, cello, and guitar players occupied the small stage area that had been set up. Later, Jan knew, the Sugarbush String Band would provide bluegrass music for dancing in the flat meadow.

"Hey, stranger." Bob slipped an arm about her waist as he joined her, fresh off a shift collecting tickets for the corn maze. "How you doing?"

"Good," Jan said. "I think everything's going fine."

"I think everything's going great," Bob corrected. "Every time I turn around, someone's singing your praises for stepping in and pulling this off at the last minute."

Jan blushed. "It was pretty well organized by the time I came on the scene," she disclaimed.

"Even so," Bob said, "you pulled all the last-minute strings together. And you can't deny there would not have been such a great corn maze without you."

She laughed. "Okay, I'll accept that one as a personal success. Oh, look." She pointed. "I see Nathan and Elaine."

Elaine was waving as she neared them. After exchanging greetings and congratulating Jan on how well the festival appeared to be going, Elaine drew her cousin aside and updated Jan on her conversation with Mrs. Burgess. "There's no way we're going to be able to speak to the board president anytime soon," she concluded.

"At least not without the police formally requesting an interview, I imagine," Jan guessed.

Elaine nodded. "Even then, it probably wouldn't be helpful. And Mrs. Burgess herself doesn't seem to know anything about the check."

Nathan stepped over to the cousins and touched Elaine's elbow. "It's almost time for the charity auction," he said.

The traditional charity auction at Harvest Home usually featured five items solicited from community businesses. Before each item was auctioned off, the donor revealed what local charity the proceeds would support. It was a popular event always planned for five o'clock since the crowds swelled in advance of dinner and the evening's entertainment.

As the four of them meandered toward the stage where the auctioneer was about to replace the folk music, Elaine stopped dead in her tracks. "Alex!" she said. "Hello."

"Hi, Elaine, hi, Jan. You remember my wife, Christa?"

"Of course. Hello. How's the little one doing?" Jan peered in at the bundled infant sleeping in a front-facing baby carrier on her chest.

"Wonderfully," Christa said. "We had a doctor's appointment last week and he gained one pound, seven ounces."

"Any news?" Alex asked before the women could enthuse about the baby any more.

Elaine shook her head. "We're still working on it." Discussing Alex's problems in a public place was hardly a good idea.

"My family set up a GoFundMe page online to help us pay the hospital for all the expenses of the baby's stay. They raised enough for us to cover the bills, and there's even some left for his future medical needs. Isn't that great? So now, no matter what happens..." Christa's lips trembled as she trailed off, but the young mother made a valiant effort to be positive.

"What a thoughtful thing to do," Jan said softly.

"Yeah," Alex said, and there was a distinct note of defeat in his tone, "except that, still, no one can vouch for the fact that Mr. Burgess authorized me to write that check for myself."

"Wait until the end of next week," Elaine said.

Alex blinked. "What? Why?"

"Can you give us a little more time?" she asked.

Awareness—and a glimmer of hope—crept into his eyes. "Of course. What are—?"

"Maybe nothing," Elaine said. "But I promise you, we haven't stopped trying."

Alex closed his eyes for a brief moment. "Thank you," he said in a huskier-than-normal voice. Christa sent them a wordless smile, though her eyes were filled with tears.

As the couple walked away, Jan said with confidence, "He didn't do it."

"I agree." Elaine turned and clasped Nathan's hand. "We'd better get over to the auction. Jan, you have to reveal the charity our quilt proceeds will go to."

THEY ALL TURNED and walked rapidly to the staging area. Jan headed for the steps at the side of the stage so she could get onstage quickly when her turn arrived, while Bob, Elaine, and Nathan stayed on the edge of the crowd.

"Back in a minute," Bob murmured before slipping away, just as Nathan and Elaine reached a good vantage point.

"Elaine Willard and Nathan Culver, is that you?" A squeaky female voice called their names.

Looking around, Elaine saw a girl—woman now—who had been in their graduating class. A tiny sprite of a thing with razored silver hair, giant hoop earrings, and flaming red lipstick, Laura Hood was her name, but everyone had called her by her nickname. "Hi, Lala, how are you? How long has it been?"

"Hey, Lala," Nathan said. "Good to see you."

"Good to see you too," their classmate answered. "It's been a long time. I live in San Francisco, and I don't get home for the class reunions," Lala said, her eyes moving back and forth between them, "so it's been a long time. My mother's still living. Said you came home after your husband passed away. Sorry for your loss."

"Thank you," Elaine said. "My cousin Jan—remember her?—and I opened a tearoom in Lancaster. It's called Tea for Two. You should come by sometime."

"Oh, I think my mother's been there," Lala said. "I will." She gestured at their clasped hands. "What's this? I never hear the good dirt."

Nathan shrugged, grinning. "What's it look like?"

"Looks like there could be a wedding in the future!" Lala crowed.

Elaine grinned. She looked at Nathan, who was grinning too, although a deep-red flush appeared above the collar of his sport shirt. She shrugged, holding his gaze with her own. "You never know." It was a rather astonishing moment, she realized. She didn't feel awkward; she didn't feel pressured. And she hoped Nathan didn't either.

"All right, ladies and gentlemen, let's get this show on the road," the auctioneer boomed, his voice amplified to drown out nearly everything else in the vicinity. "Welcome to the Seventy-seventh Chickadee Lake Harvest Home Festival, and to our annual charity auction. The first item up for auction is a KitchenAid Artisan three-and-a-half-quart tilt-head stand mixer donated by Kitchen Caboodlin' in Penzance. Folks, this little beauty retails for $300, but we're hoping you'll be generous with your bids as this is a charity auction. And here's Louella Manier to tell us what charity Kitchen Caboodlin' will donate the proceeds of this auction to."

The auctioneer handed off the microphone to the business owner, who loudly declared, "The Central Maine Humane Society."

There was a general cheer and clapping, loudest in one part of the crowd that Elaine suspected was made up of volunteers and staff from the animal shelter. Almost immediately, the auctioneer began his patter. "Who'll give me $100? Who'll give me...," and the auction was off to a good start as bid cards shot into the air right and left. When the bidding ended, the stand mixer had brought in almost $400 for the humane society.

The second item was a week in an oceanfront home on Cape Cod, donated by a roofing company whose owner owned the home. That went for significantly more, and a third item, a playhouse handmade by the employees of a cabinetry company, brought in nearly a grand.

There were only two items left now. Next up was a set of weathered wooden barn doors reclaimed from an old barn that had been taken down. Bidding over those was fierce and hectic. Two bidders at the end sent the price soaring and the crowd hooted and hollered when the final gavel came down.

Elaine swallowed nervously as three auction workers came forward to the edge of the stage with the harvest quilt. Carefully, they unfolded it and held it up to be displayed.

"Wow," Nathan said as a murmur of awe ran through the crowd. "You guys pulled it off." He shook his head admiringly. "You really pulled it off."

"We did, didn't we?" Elaine asked, beaming.

The muted autumn shades of the fabrics glowed in the late-day sunlight that dappled the open-air stage. They'd been right to make it so big, she thought. It was magnificent.

"Our final auction entry is a harvest quilt donated by Jan Blake and Elaine Cook, owners of Lancaster's Tea for Two tearoom." He gave the quilt's measurements. "The pattern for the quilt was created by Camille Lapole, who also pieced it and finished it. The quilting was done by nearly two dozen quilters during a quilting bee held at the tearoom last week. Jan, do you want to come up here and tell us who your charity is?"

Jan ascended the steps to the stage and stood blinking out at the crowd. She smiled. "Everyone who worked on this was a volunteer," she said. "It was a true labor of love, and we offer the proceeds from it in that spirit to... Homes for Maine's Heroes."

A spate of spontaneous clapping followed her words.

"This thing is really special," the auctioneer said. "Ladies and gents, get your arms oiled to hold those bid cards high."

Once again, the early bids practically tumbled over each other as the price went up and up. Slowly people dropped out as they passed the $300, then the $400 and $500 mark. Nearly as quickly went $600, then $700, and there were still four bidders in the game, Elaine saw. She identified two people bidding in front of her, and looking around, she spotted another back to her left. Where was the fourth one?

"Who's the other bidder?" she asked Bob and Nathan.

Bob shook his head, intent on the bidding. His arms were tightly crossed. He was nervous for Jan's sake, Elaine thought with a warm swell of feeling.

"It looks like it might be an anonymous bidder," Nathan said. "Someone from the back table is bidding." The back table was where bidders had registered and acquired their bid cards.

"What do you mean, anonymous?" Elaine whispered. Bidding had stalled for a moment at $950, and one of the bidders up front dropped out.

"Someone placed a bid at the table and gave them a maximum limit," Nathan said. "They're authorized to be that person's agent and to bid up to that amount for them."

The bid went up again as the other person up front flashed his bid card. Elaine watched in disbelief as it rose over $1,000, $1,100, and up to $1,225.

She pressed both hands to her mouth. "Oh my," she whispered. They'd had high hopes of raising $600 to $700, but they'd prepared themselves for a sale in the $400 to $500 range.

"Anybody twelve and a half? Twelve and a half, twelve and a half? I'm waiting for twelve and a half, the table in the back has it at twelve and a quarter, do I hear twelve and a half? Going once at one thousand two hundred twenty-five, do I have a twelve and a half? Going once, going twice at twelve twenty-five, will you give me twelve and a half?" The auctioneer paused just long enough for the final counter-bidder to shake his head regretfully.

"Sold!" he called.

CHAPTER TWENTY-ONE

Elaine gasped as the gavel came down.

"Sold to the table in the back for $1,225. Congratulations, Tea for Two, and thanks to all who participated in our auction today," the auctioneer boomed.

"I wonder who bought the quilt?" Nathan looked after the auction hands who had carefully refolded the quilt, slipped it inside the giant plastic bag Jan had provided to transport it, and were delivering it to the workers at the table at the back. One of them received it and carefully walked away as others began to tear down the temporary auction setup.

"I imagine we'll find out eventually," Bob said.

"I'm not sure I care," Elaine said, "except that we should probably write them a thank-you note. Over $1200 for HMH! I can't believe it."

As the words slipped out of her mouth, she was surprised to see Mitch Ackerly approaching. He had a small girl perched in one arm. Mitch's free hand held that of a fragile-looking blonde, and on her other side was a tall man with iron-gray hair and a strong jaw. The older man had another little girl trotting along clinging to his hand.

Mitch must have heard what she said, because he gave her a wide smile. "Hi, Elaine. Great job," he told her. "That was amazing. I was tempted to bid, but my wife said it wouldn't really go with our décor."

The delicate-looking blonde at his side raised her eyebrows. "Well, it wouldn't." She extended a hand to Elaine. "Bettina Dacourt-Vallerand."

"Sorry," Mitch said. "I should have introduced you. Honey, this is Elaine Cook, who's been volunteering in the office for the past two weeks. Elaine, my wife, and this is my father-in-law, Lloyd Vallerand."

Elaine introduced Nathan, who greeted them politely. Bob had vanished, probably headed up front to where Jan was still mobbed by people offering congratulations.

"And these are my munchkins." Mitch's pride couldn't be faked. He glanced lovingly from one child to the other as he introduced the children to Elaine.

"Did I see you talking to Alex earlier?" Mitch asked. "I was pretty sure I saw Christa and him with you, but by the time I got through the crowd all of you were gone."

Elaine nodded. She hadn't had any idea that Mitch had observed her talking to Alex, and the thought made her extremely uncomfortable. "Yes," she said. "We have a mutual friend."

"I didn't realize you knew him," Mitch said. "If you see him again, please tell him I'm thinking of him," Mitch said.

"Of course," Elaine managed.

"Look, Bettina." Lloyd Vallerand spoke. "There's Jarrott Rugle, your high school sweetheart. I'm sure he'd love to see you." Lloyd, to Elaine's surprise, glared at Mitch. Was this the way the super-rich behaved in public, or was Lloyd simply ruder than most?

Bettina's face lit up, and she looked in the direction her father had indicated. "Nice to have met you, er, Ellen," she said absently.

Mitch took his child's hand as his father-in-law and wife turned and walked off without another word. Nathan deftly changed the subject, asking Mitch's older daughter about her favorite things she had seen at the festival.

But Elaine was watching Lloyd, who was still within earshot. He had leaned over to Bettina as they walked away and said slyly, "Jarrott is newly single, you know. And more successful than ever." Bettina looked up at her father as they walked and said something that Elaine couldn't make out.

Elaine rejoined the conversation in front of her and noticed that Mitch's face was flushed with what Elaine suspected was humiliation, and his mouth twisted wryly. "Well, it was lovely to speak to you both. Come on, girls. I promised you some funnel cake, didn't I?" To Elaine, he said, "Nice to have seen you 'out in the wild.'" He paused. "And I really am sorry I missed Alex. I haven't seen him since the day they escorted him out of the office."

Elaine nearly bit her tongue trying to keep from responding. The first week she'd gone to HMH, she distinctly remembered Mitch telling her he hadn't been in the office that day.

Mitch glanced at Nathan. "Nice to meet you."

"And you," Nathan said.

"See you Monday," Elaine said to Mitch, her head spinning.

"So, you're positive Mitch lied to you." Jan said. It was Sunday afternoon, and the cousins were planning menus for the upcoming week and reviewing their tea selections. They'd just finished lunch after attending a special harvest-themed service at Lancaster Community Church, where the crowd had been swelled by many visiting family members who'd come to town for the Harvest Home Festival.

"I'm positive. I've been trying to figure out what that means since yesterday," Elaine said. "Does it mean he's guilty? Or is there something else going on?"

"That's the question," Jan said. "And that ugly little scene you witnessed between his father-in-law and wife was also really, really weird."

"It was," Elaine agreed. "I felt terribly sorry for Mitch as well as those dear little ones."

A squeaking sound interrupted their discussion.

"What was that?" Elaine looked around.

Jan rose. "I don't know, but it sounded like it came from the pantry." She walked across the room and reached for the doorknob, realizing as she did so that the pantry door was slightly ajar.

Another squeaking sound rent the air, and the door opened a little.

Jan stepped back with a surprised exclamation—and who strolled into the kitchen but a familiar furry friend.

"Earl Grey!" Jan was astonished. "What are you doing? How did you get in here?"

The cat made a trilling meow in answer as he walked across the kitchen.

"And you can't stay," Elaine said firmly. "The health department would have our license if we started serving cat-hair muffins."

Earl Grey ignored this observation. In one surprisingly lithe move, he leaped up onto the kitchen island and investigated Jan's mug of tea. The mug rocked dangerously but righted itself as he withdrew his muzzle.

Elaine rose and grabbed the cat, then tucked him firmly beneath one arm. "Come on, pal, out you go."

"How did he get in there?"

Jan yanked open the pantry door. At the back of the pantry was a small round window with six sides. Shelves were built all around it. There was an inner latch on the glass and a little handle one could use to crank the window open a few inches.

"The window's not latched," Jan said. "And Earl Grey must have figured that out. The crank is giving way, so when it's opened, it falls almost all the way closed—but not quite. See?" She demonstrated the loose window latch for Elaine. "All he had to do was jump up on the back of the Adirondack chair out there and paw it open."

"I can't believe that big cat squeezed through that tiny opening!" Elaine said from behind her.

Jan laughed. "He's got ingenuity, I'll give him that."

"He may have ingenuity," Elaine said, "but we've got duct tape. I'll close the window from the outside so he can't get in again, and tomorrow we'll get someone over here to replace that latch."

CHAPTER TWENTY-TWO

Monday was the start of Elaine's final week at Homes for Maine's Heroes, and she couldn't have been more anxious to be there.

When she parked her car—finally repaired after the airbags had deployed—and entered the office that morning, Ted smiled and actually rose from his desk to hug her, and Elaine could barely contain her surprise at Ted's friendliness. She knew he had been warming up to her, but this was a new level. "Penny told me about the quilt," he said. "I can't believe you're donating $1200 plus to HMH."

Penny came through the door from the back and delivered a hug of her own. "I was at the festival yesterday, but I didn't get to talk to you. Congratulations and thank you!"

Elaine grinned. "Of course! I hardly could believe my eyes and ears when the bid kept going up and up and up."

"Who bought it?" Ted asked. "I think they deserve a huge thank-you from HMH."

"I don't know," Elaine was forced to admit. "It was an anonymous bidder who hasn't revealed herself or himself yet."

"Well, if you ever figure it out, will you let me know so I can write a note?"

"Absolutely," Elaine said.

Around ten, R.J. came breezing in from a breakfast meeting and congratulated her on the quilt's sale. He and his wife had heard about it from friends at their church yesterday.

"It's terrific," he told Elaine. "Make sure you give Ted the donor's name for a thank-you. We're all on edge about donation acknowledgments for taxes now since the board vice president found out Jean Briggs hadn't gotten one." He made a wry face. "Which turned out to be a good thing, since Alex was stealing us blind." He shook his head. "I really liked that boy. Hard to believe."

"Mr. Cole, the vice president, was the one who initially found out about the missing tax letter?" Elaine asked carefully. "I thought Mitch raised the alarm."

"He did," R.J. said. "But Jean Briggs talked to Idris Cole first, and he sent her to Mitch."

"I see." And she did.

That afternoon, Penny had a dental appointment and left at three thirty, but Elaine wanted to work a few minutes more, so she stayed. As she gathered her things, she heard Mitch's voice down the hallway, and it was clear he wasn't speaking to a donor. She stopped cold.

"Don't," she heard him say in a pleading tone. "Bettina, don't take the kids anywhere. Wait until I get home. We'll figure it out."

There was a pause, and when Mitch spoke again, his voice was angry. "Two can play this game, Bettina. Don't forget I can make sure you never see our children again too. Is that really what you want?"

Elaine heard him push back from his rolling chair and his footsteps moved toward the door. She pressed herself against the side wall of the office, around the corner, hoping Mitch hadn't seen her.

"I'm taking off," he said to Ted in a far more normal tone of voice. "See you tomorrow."

"Goodbye," Ted echoed.

Elaine felt adrenaline rushing through her.

She waited, pressed against the wall where she was out of sight, for what felt like a long time. Outside the window, she heard the harsh call of a bird. From the front office, there was only silence. Ted, presumably, was still there. He was usually the last one out of the office. Mitch appeared to have left.

Cautiously, Elaine stuck her head out. There was no one in the hall. She headed quickly toward the office door. But as she did, she saw a file folder on the hall floor.

Had Mitch dropped it as he was leaving? She bent and scooped up the folder, then carried it toward Mitch's office at the far end of the hallway.

She took it into the office and laid it on Mitch's desk, but as she did, a paper slipped out of one side. It looked like a deposit ticket. Heart pounding, she flipped open the folder.

It was indeed a deposit ticket, but it was for an account at the Waterville bank Ted had gone to. And the account name was listed as HMH.

There were three checks listed, with a total amount of $4,000, and it was dated from May. Elaine began to put the ticket back into the folder, but when she opened the file, she saw a second deposit ticket from the same bank: total amount, $2,500, dated from July. At this point, there was no denying it: she'd found her embezzler.

And now she even knew why he'd framed Alex: Mitch had been trying to keep his marriage afloat with the company's funds, and when his wife's aunt mentioned her missing tax donor letter to the vice president of the board, he realized he was going to be caught.

Quickly, Elaine's fingers shuffled aside four deposit tickets. She couldn't help herself. She looked at the open file folder before her, lifting the deposit tickets. Below them were documents clearly relating to a business account for a company called Having More Hope.

Her heart sped up. With a jolt, she realized she was looking at the dummy corporation—wasn't that what it was called?—that Mitch must have set up to divert funds from Homes for Maine's Heroes.

Elaine called Jan, then put the phone on speaker. When her cousin answered, she said tensely, "I have news."

"So do I!" Jan announced. "You're not going to believe this, but I found the missing thread. It was right where I put it—which may be the dumbest thing I've ever done. I stuck it in the pantry behind a stack of the new tea we just ordered. I just found it as I was fixing the window. I remember thinking at the time I'd remember where it was, but clearly my memory wasn't up to the task."

"That's great," Elaine said quietly, still looking at the file. "Listen to me. I'm in Mitch's office. He dropped a folder and left, and when I brought it back to his office, I saw deposit tickets and a fake bank account. Jan, it's been Mitch all along. He's been depositing pilfered checks into another bank, into an account belonging to a dummy corporation with the same initials. HMH. It wasn't a one-time thing either."

Jan gasped. "Are you kidding? That's exactly what we need to take to the police."

"Yes, I think it is." She needed to close the folder and get out of Mitch's office before she finished this conversation. "Hold on a minute, okay?"

"Sure."

Elaine set her phone down beside the folder and began to try to put the deposit tickets back in the order in which she'd found them.

"Looking for something, Elaine?" a masculine voice asked from the doorway.

CHAPTER TWENTY-TWO

Elaine gasped and whipped around.

"Hi, Mitch," she said, striving for calm. She stood, grasping the edge of the desk to pull herself up and using the opportunity to nudge some papers lying on the desk over the phone. "I was just—uh, I didn't expect you back. You dropped a file folder in the hallway, so I brought it back to your office."

"I know exactly what you're doing," he said, his voice quivering. "You're snooping around looking for some way to tie me to the theft of the checks. You've been doing it all along. I don't know who you think you are, but this is none of your business."

"Appears to be none of yours either," Elaine said, sounding much more composed than she felt.

He shook his head. "I knew when I saw you talking to Alex yesterday that I had a problem. Actually, I knew before that. I caught you looking at that list on my desk a week ago, and you were a little too interested." He closed the office door with a quick shove of one polished leather loafer and walked to the bookshelf nearby.

Confused and startled, Elaine froze. She thought about making a run for it, but Mitch was between her and the closed door. She stood waiting to see what he would do.

Mitch pulled a book from the shelf—and immediately, Elaine knew she was in trouble. It wasn't a book at all. It was a box cleverly designed to look like a book. And Mitch lifted a small black revolver out of it. Slowly, he pointed the gun at her. "I really wish you hadn't done this."

"Why do you have a pistol hidden in your office?" she blurted. "Are you going to shoot me while Ted's still here? Not the wisest idea," she said.

"I'll do whatever I need to do to keep your nose out of my business," he said with a small shake of his head.

Elaine eyed the pistol he was carelessly holding. Everything came together in that moment. The missing lug nuts. The note. The person in front of her, the person who had threatened her before and was threatening her now, was a desperate man. A man about to lose his family.

"Don't do this, Mitch. You'll just make everything worse."

Mitch tightened his jaw and stepped closer to Elaine. He held the gun a little higher, but Elaine could see a crack in Mitch's resolve. "I had no choice. You saw my wife, my father-in-law. The money I made on my own was never going to be enough. I had to do something. My kids mean too much to me, and my wife has already threatened to leave me for her ex. She recently told me she regretted marrying me before she even finished saying 'I do.' She wants total custody."

"I'm so sorry," Elaine said, in hopes of diffusing his anger. She couldn't help but think it wasn't just money that made

Bettina want to leave, but a clear degree of mental instability on Mitch's part. But she also had seen that Bettina was certainly materialistic and seemed to be getting enough pressure of her own from her father. Regardless, the path Mitch had chosen was foolish and dishonorable. "Mitch," Elaine continued, "surely you know this isn't a permanent solution. What were you going to do when you got caught?"

"Shut up," Mitch said, lunging toward her.

JAN NEARLY DROPPED her phone when she heard the male voice ask, "Looking for something, Elaine?"

She gasped and then immediately clapped her hand over her mouth. Was there a chance Elaine's phone wasn't in plain sight? Hastily she hit mute so there would be no chance of a sound from her end adding to Elaine's troubles.

Her heart was pounding. What should she do? As she listened to the conversation, she leaped across the room and grabbed the house phone. Quickly, she called Dan, her fingers trembling.

"Hey, Jan," Dan said. "You have news?"

"We've got trouble," she blurted. "Mitch Ackerly just walked in on Elaine searching his desk, and he's got a gun!"

"A gun?" Dan's voice immediately dropped into what she thought of as his "no nonsense" law enforcement tone. "Jan, call 9-1-1 right now and tell them it's an emergency, that a man at HMH may have a hostage. That'll get them moving really fast, and then you can explain the rest. Make sure you tell them an armed off-duty officer will meet them there. I'm headed over there now." She heard a brief jingle of keys, and then Dan disconnected.

Fingers shaking, Jan dialed 9-1-1, then shared all the information she could with the dispatcher.

"Thank you, ma'am," the dispatcher said. "Please stay on the line."

"I have to go," Jan blurted. "Please, please send someone. Quick!"

"Mrs. Blake, we don't want—"

But it was too late to hear what the dispatcher didn't want. Jan ended the call and grabbed her phone, listening closely as she grabbed her keys and rushed out the back door.

MITCH LUNGED, BUT he wasn't going for Elaine as she had at first thought. He reached past her and snatched the bank papers Elaine had set down. "I'm not getting caught. Who are the authorities going to believe? Some dumb old tea lady or a man of my repute?"

Elaine swallowed. "Well, the evidence is right here. These bank papers clearly show that you've been embezzling from HMH." she added. "They may not believe 'some dumb old tea lady,' but the evidence doesn't lie."

A door hinge squawked, and footsteps came along the hallway in their direction. A knock sounded, and the door swung open. "I'm taking off now," Ted said "Did you want this door shut?"

"No," Mitch said casually, holding the gun out of Ted's sight. "You can leave it open. See you tomorrow."

Ted looked uncertainly from Mitch to Elaine. "Is everything okay?"

"Everything's fine," Mitch said quickly. "Elaine was just helping me with some odds and ends of paperwork."

The young man's face cleared. "All right then. See you tomorrow."

"See you tomorrow," Elaine echoed, not sure whether to scream or comply. If she made known what Mitch was doing, would he hold Ted hostage too?

Elaine stood in wooden silence as Ted's footsteps receded, listening as the door to the front office opened, and Elaine breathed again. At least Ted would be out of there if Mitch started shooting.

Elaine thought about her phone. She could only hope that Jan was still on the line, and that she had called the police. In the meantime, she needed to keep Mitch talking—the longer, the better. If he took her somewhere else, Dan might not be able to locate her. "It sounds like you've been under a lot of pressure, Mitch," she said, keeping her voice low and quiet.

"Do you have any idea what it's like to live with someone who expects you to be so much more than you are?"

Elaine watched him, giving her head a tiny shake. She was terrified he was going to turn the gun on her—or even on himself. "No," she said quietly. "It sounds difficult."

"Difficult? Ha! I'm just an average guy," Mitch said. "Just an average guy with a decent job. I fell for the wrong woman. I know that now." He looked miserable. "You have no idea what pressure is," he told her. "Have you ever gotten a credit card bill that you can't pay? For obscenely expensive designer shoes and purses?" he added bitterly. "One pair she's never even worn. I checked."

"So you set up the fake account for the deposits. Ted never had any idea that wasn't a real HMH account he was making deposits to, did he?"

Mitch grinned and shook his head. "Good old Ted was clueless."

"And you removed the donations you stole from the spreadsheet after Ted entered them. And you were smart enough to send thank-you letters from the real HMH, knowing the chances an auditor would ever check on a charitable donation like that are practically nil."

"Pretty perfect plan, isn't it," Mitch said, a mix of bravado and sadness in his voice.

"What went wrong?" Elaine asked.

Mitch sniffed aggressively. "I did everything right, except this one single time." Mitch shook his head at himself. "I forgot to send out one of the letters, and to Bettina's officious old aunt, of all people. That's what caused all this trouble. When Idris Cole told me Jean Briggs reported not getting a letter, I was sure I was about to be caught."

"So you framed Alex by hiding those checks in his desk," she hazarded, still stalling for time. How many minutes had passed?

"Right," Mitch said. "The check in his car was a total bonus. I didn't even know he had borrowed money from the company until Burgess called me later in the day on his way out of town and told me to note it in the books."

"And of course you didn't," she said. "Did you have anything to do with the missing lumber?" It was the only thing she could think of to ask him that might keep him talking.

Mitch looked blank for a moment. Then he laughed. "What would I do with lumber? No, that was an honest error on the part of the company. They misread the quantity and delivered the wrong amount. Why? Did you think maybe R.J. did it?" He chuckled. Then his face sobered. "I really hate to do this, Elaine, but we have to go now."

"Where?"

Mitch gestured with the gun. "Enough chatting. Let's go."

CHAPTER TWENTY-THREE

Jan drove like a maniac, continuing to listen to the conversation coming from her cell phone. Just as she reached the edge of Waterville, she heard Mitch's final order. "Let's go."

"No," she breathed, fighting for calm. She careened around the corner toward HMH—and stomped on the brakes. There were four cop cars parked in different locations along the street. None of the locations, she realized, could be seen from the building. Dan stood beside a man with a bullhorn who looked to be in charge. Officers with their hands on their weapons were creeping carefully along the blind edges of nearby buildings, or, in one case, slipping from tree to tree to get closer to the building. Another officer was hustling away a slight young man whom Jan recognized from the security footage as Ted Harrington.

A movement at the door of the building caught her attention. Elaine emerged, still alive and looking unharmed. Jan almost moaned aloud with relief, until she realized that right behind Elaine came Mitch Ackerly, with one hand conspicuously in his pocket.

What, she wondered wildly, were the police going to do? If they frightened him, Mitch might accidently pull the trigger.

Just then, two burly officers sprinted from the bushes at either side of the front door. One tackled Mitch, yanking his arm straight up into the air before slamming him to the ground. The other dragged Elaine to the side and hustled her away. No shots marred the stillness of the late afternoon.

Jan threw the Toyota into park and scrambled out of the car. She ran headlong toward her cousin, heedless of the officers shouting at her to stop.

"Family! She's family!" Dan was yelling.

The officer who had pulled Elaine to safety was helping her get her bearings, saying gruffly, "I apologize for any roughness, ma'am, we—"

"Elaine!" Jan skidded to a halt and threw her arms around her cousin. "Are you all right?" She had to stop and wait to speak until she was sure she wouldn't burst into sobs.

"I think so," Elaine said shakily. "This officer was protecting me."

And then Dan was there, kneeling before them both. He placed one arm around Jan and one around Elaine. "That was cutting it a little too close." Jan was astonished to see that he had to stop and swallow. "This is far, far above and beyond anything I ever expected when I asked you to help Alex," he confessed. "I'm so sorry I put you in danger."

"Dan." Elaine stopped him. "You did not put me in danger. I did that when I made a poor decision to snoop around in an office where I didn't belong."

All three of them turned to watch as Mitch, who had been handcuffed and read his rights, was loaded into a squad car for a ride to police headquarters.

"I want to go talk to the case investigators," Dan said, "and share our end of things. They may want to interview one or both of you, but I'll ask them to wait until tomorrow."

He put a hand under Elaine's elbow and Jan took the other, and she turned toward the car with one of them on each side, testing all her limbs.

"A soak in a hot tub might help with a few of the bruises I'm going to have." She cleared her throat. "Thanks to both of you, I'm just fine otherwise."

That silenced them all for a moment as everyone relived the frightening moments. Jan suspected Dan and Elaine were imagining, as she couldn't stop doing, how much worse it could have been.

"All right," she finally said. "Why don't I drive you home?"

"I don't even have my handbag," Elaine protested.

"I'll have an officer get your things and bring your car by later," Dan said. "You let Jan take you home now."

"And you'd better use my phone to call Nathan and Sasha," Jan said to her cousin. "You know how word spreads. They'll be frantic if they hear about this from someone else."

Elaine did not go back to Homes for Maine's Heroes.

Penny called her that evening to tell her she didn't need to come in, that they had made such great progress on their presentations that she could easily finish them up herself. She sent along Sally's and R.J.'s regards as well. "They called me as soon as they heard what happened, and they wanted me to let you know how thankful they are that you're okay. And Ted is so upset that he didn't realize what was going on in Mitch's office when he came by today. He hopes you'll forgive him."

"That's sweet," Elaine said. She would miss her "coworkers" from HMH. "Please tell poor Ted not to worry about it since I'm fine. And have them all stop by the tearoom sometime and say hello."

On Tuesday, the tearoom was abuzz with the story of Elaine's escape, and she was forced to spend long periods of time in the office or the kitchen to avoid having to repeat the events to every fascinated soul who came by.

Dan called shortly after lunch. "Charlotte and I would like to take you two and Bob and Nathan to dinner tonight to thank you for what you did for Alex." Although Elaine tried to demur, Dan was insistent. "You won't regret it," he said. "I've already talked to Bob and to Nathan. We'll pick you up around six."

Elaine smiled. "All right. Thank you."

Dan had made reservations at the Odyssey, a restaurant that had recently opened in Lancaster. To Jan and Elaine's surprise, Alex and Christa DeRone were waiting for them there.

"We can't stay for dinner," Alex said, "because Miles gets pretty fussy in the evenings. But we wanted to thank you in person for everything you did to help us. Are you sure we can't pay you?"

Elaine shook her head. "Absolutely not."

"Just send new business to the tearoom when you can," Jan quipped, grinning.

"Absolutely," Christa said. She had tears in her eyes. "You will never know how deeply grateful we are for your help, and we're both so thankful you, Elaine, were not injured yesterday." Alex brought a beribboned gift bag piled high with green and lavender tissue as she continued. "We hope you'll accept this token of our thanks and think of the way you changed our lives every time you look at it."

"It" was a stunning hand-crafted glass star. Made of ten faceted diamonds of glass soldered into a flat bronze framework, the star was nearly twelve inches high and wide.

Elaine gave an involuntary gasp of pleasure as Jan held up the stunning piece. The facets caught the light and arrested the attention of others dining around them. "That's gorgeous," she said. "Thank you so much."

"We'll hang it in a window," Jan said, "where it will catch the light. It's lovely. And we'll think of you every time we see it."

Christa beamed. "I hoped you'd like it."

Alex offered first Jan, and then Elaine, a handshake and a warm hug. "Thank you again. I heard from the vice president of the board today, and I start back to work tomorrow."

"Oh, that's terrific news," Elaine said. It was the best outcome they could have wished for on the day Dan had stood, stricken, in their kitchen as he learned his friend had been suspended on suspicion of theft.

Alex and Christa left soon after, and the party of six settled down to enjoy a good meal.

"Here's to friendship," Dan said, holding aloft his water glass.

"To friendship," they all echoed.

WHEN DINNER WAS over, Jan, Bob, Elaine, and Nathan headed back to the tearoom. As they took off their coats, Jan said, "Do you guys want to come upstairs and catch the evening news?"

"That would be nice," Bob said, "but before we do, I have to say something."

They were all standing in the foyer, and Jan noticed Elaine looked as puzzled as she was. Nathan, on the other hand, was smiling slightly.

"Give me one second," Bob said. He turned and went into the west parlor, emerging a moment later with a long jewelry box in one hand and—

"Our quilt!" Jan was amazed. "How did you get our quilt?"

Bob was smiling as he handed the bagged quilt to her. "I bought it," he said. "I knew how much you loved the finished product, and I wanted you to have it."

Jan felt tears press at the backs of her eyes. She hugged the quilt to her chest and wrapped an arm around Bob's neck to kiss him. "Thank you so much."

She looked at Elaine. "Where shall we put this? We have to display it somehow."

Bob cleared his throat. "Well, as to that, I had an idea." He extended the jewelry box to her.

Nathan was openly grinning now, and Jan realized he must have been in on hiding the items in the house before they left for dinner.

"What is this?" she asked suspiciously. "It's not my birthday."

Bob smiled. "Open it."

Jan handed the quilt to Elaine and took the box. Expecting a necklace from its shape, she flipped open the hinged lid.

It wasn't a necklace. And Bob was taking the box from her nerveless fingers and untying the flashing diamond ring from a set of keys. She was too overcome to think.

Bob knelt, taking her left hand in his. "Jan Blake, you are my other half, the part that completes me. We are not children. We have loved and lost, and we've been fortunate enough to find love again. Will you marry me?"

Jan looked down at him, at the silver at his temples and the crinkles at the corners of his warm brown eyes, at the love that shone from them, her tears overflowing. She couldn't believe they were at this point again, now that he'd moved back from Baltimore. But this time, there was nothing to complicate her answer. "Oh yes," she said. "Yes, yes, yes! Of course I'll marry you."

Elaine and Nathan clapped as Bob slipped the pretty diamond ring onto her finger. "It's a round brilliant-cut with step-cut baguette accents at each side," he said, anxiously gauging her expression. "If you don't like it, we can—"

"I love it!" Jan closed her free hand protectively over it. "Don't you dare take my ring away."

They all laughed.

"But what are the keys for?" Jan asked, truly perplexed.

"These," Bob said, lifting them from the box, "are the keys to our future home. If, of course, you like it."

She was caught off guard. "But how can I move away from the tearoom?" she asked, only half joking.

"That's the beauty of this particular home," Bob said. "This set of keys opens the doors to a very special house." He tugged her to the front door and threw it open wide. Pointing across the street at the old Victorian in the front yard, he said, "We'd be living right there."

"And this quilt," Elaine said, coming to place the treasure in Jan's arms, "will look absolutely spectacular in that house."

Jan just shook her head. "I can't believe this," she said. "When I woke up this morning, I thought my life was perfect. We'd helped solve Dan's crime, and Elaine was safe, and we had a home and business we loved. But now it's even more perfect!" She flung her arms around Bob. "Oh, I love you. Can we go over there and look through it right now? And talk about remodeling the kitchen?"

Bob laughed. "I assumed that was a given." He took her hand—the one with her stunning new ring on it—and led her out of the house.

As HER COUSIN and her fiancé flew down the steps and ran across the street, hand in hand and laughing like children, Elaine watched them go with a smile. "Ah," she said, "that was perfect, wasn't it?"

Nathan put his arms around her from behind. "It was pretty special," he agreed. "I think it's a good solution for them. She can still work here almost as easily as if she lived right upstairs."

Elaine leaned back into the solid strength of the man she loved, content for now. The future would take care of itself, she decided. Jan was getting married. Her daughter was getting married. There would be many plans to make and many joys to share. She didn't need to think any further than that for today.

"I think so too," she agreed, turning in his arms and lifting her face for his kiss.

ABOUT THE AUTHOR

Anne Marie Rodgers has written more than twenty novels for Guideposts and nearly five dozen stories in her twenty-five-year publishing career, including a number of best-sellers and award winners. Anne Marie is deeply committed to animal rescue and wildlife rehabilitation and has become a bat care specialist in her Savannah, Georgia, community. One of her greatest joys in life is her growing family, which includes two grandchildren and another on the way.

From the Tea for Two Kitchen
Jan's Festive Pumpkin Log
Makes one 9" log

Loaf:

- 3 eggs
- ½ cup canned pumpkin
- 1 cup sugar
- 1 tsp. baking soda
- ½ tsp. cinnamon
- ¾ cup flour
- Confectioner's sugar to sprinkle

Filling:

- 2 T. butter
- 8 oz cream cheese, softened
- ¾ tsp. vanilla extract
- 1 cup confectioner's sugar

Preheat oven to 350°. Lay out cream cheese.

Loaf: Mix with electric mixer until well mixed: eggs, pumpkin, sugar, baking soda, cinnamon, and flour. Fit wax paper into a large cookie sheet; pour a very thin layer of mixture out. Bake for 15 minutes; remove. Lay a clean tea towel on table; cover with confectioner's sugar. Turn contents of cookie sheet onto tea towel, and roll it up gently in the tea towel before it cools. After it cools, remove wax paper and trim edges. Cool until filling is mixed.

Filling: Combine butter, cream cheese, vanilla extract and powdered sugar; mix until smooth. Spread on pumpkin cake.

Carefully, leaving towel flat, roll cake into a cylinder. Freeze a minimum of three hours.

Cut while frozen; serve slices after 15-30 minutes.

Read on for an exciting sneak peek
into the next volume of Tearoom Mysteries!

In Too Deep

by Elizabeth Adams

"Grandma, aren't you going to have a s'more?" Avery held a freshly made treat in her one hand, melted marshmallow running down her fingers. She had a stick in the other, and a wide grin on her face.

"No, thank you. Not for me," Jan said.

Avery looked at Tae, the new girl in the youth group, who stood next to her, and shrugged. Tae had already eaten most of her blackened marshmallow right off the stick, and she took another bite now before announcing, "Old people are weird."

Avery nodded her agreement, and the two girls moved off, over to where a clump of preteens were chatting on the far side of the camp fire.

Jan tried not to let the words sting. It wasn't that she didn't like s'mores. What was not to like about roasted marshmallow, graham cracker, and chocolate? What Jan didn't like was the way those twelve-year-old boys were lighting marshmallows on fire and waving the sticks around. Jan held her breath, watching as one boy pretended to push his friend into the fire and very nearly succeeded. Tommy Harp, the seminary student who was interning as a youth pastor for the semester, reached out and steadied the boy before disaster struck, and they all went on as if nothing had happened.

There was a special place in heaven for youth pastors. She didn't know how they did it. She was too old for this.

Jan met the eye of Matt McInnis, sitting on the other side of the fire, and without a word she understood that he felt the same way. Matt was a doctor back in Lancaster, and his son Anthony was in sixth grade this year. Anthony had been excited to join the youth group, so when Tommy had asked for chaperones to take the youth group on a camping trip, Matt had signed right up. And Jan was here because her granddaughter Avery was in the youth group. Tommy had recently learned that many of the kids—including Avery—had never actually been camping, despite growing up in Central Maine, and he had wanted to take the kids on a camping trip before the weather got too cold. Thirteen-year-old Avery hadn't been too keen on skipping a shower and sleeping on the ground in mid-November, so Jan—who had always loved camping in her younger days—had volunteered to go along if Avery would give it a shot. Judging by the excited way she was talking with the group of girls on the far side of the fire, she was having a good time.

Jan looked around the group of teens and preteens gathered around the campfire. They all seemed to be having a good time, actually. Everyone seemed to be talking, laughing, and generally enjoying the evening. And what wasn't to like? A clear dark sky was lit with thousands of silver sparkling stars, and the fire sent a soft golden glow over the faces, and over the tents and trees beyond. The sweet scent of pine and spruce trees carried on the cool breeze, but it was warm right here by the fire.

"All right. Who's ready for some singing?" Tommy Harp was in his mid-twenties, and though he was short, he was strong and had the sort of wide, open, face that made you believe him. He also had that overly-enthusiastic attitude that most youth pastors shared, and while the kids generally responded well to him, right now there was no competing with flaming marshmallows. But once he'd unpacked his guitar and started playing the first few notes of "Pharaoh, Pharaoh," the kids all sat down on the log benches and started to sing along. Jan had never much liked this song, but she loved that youth group kids were still singing it two generations after she had learned it at church camp.

After several silly songs, Tommy moved to slower, more worshipful tunes, and the sound of young voices lifting praise to God echoed through the trees in the still night. It struck something deep inside Jan—being out here in nature, surrounded by the majesty of His creation, hearing His children praise him... it was beautiful. Tommy led them all in prayer together before they were dismissed. As the kids stood up from the logs and headed for the tents, with plenty of giggling and shrieking, Jan paused to sprinkle dirt on the fire. It smothered slowly.

"Thanks for your help." Tommy walked up carrying a five-gallon bucket filled with water he'd hauled from the creek that ran below the campsite.

"No problem. Thank you for doing this. We need more youth events at the church, and I'm so glad you were willing to step forward and volunteer."

"I have to do an internship as part of my seminary training, and I've always had a soft spot for junior high kids," Tommy said. He had the stocky build of a wrestler, and he'd mentioned to Jan that he had been All-American in college. Jan couldn't help but think skills like that might come in handy trying to wrangle youth group kids—or a congregation. "That's when my faith really started to feel real to me, not just something that I did because my parents believed it."

Jan nodded. Junior high had been an important time in her own faith journey as well. "For me as well. And I'm hoping Avery will really develop some deeper friendships with the kids in the youth group."

"She's a good kid," Tommy said as he scooped out water with a cup and sprinkled it over the coals. "And she seems to be getting to know Tae, which is great."

"Yes." Jan wasn't sure what else to say. There wasn't anything wrong with Tae, exactly. She seemed like a nice enough kid. Tae was Bristol Payson's niece, and she had recently moved to Lancaster to live with the Paysons for a while because her parents were going through a messy divorce. Tae was a year older than Avery, and in a different grade, but she seemed even older than that somehow. More streetwise.

Jan turned the ashes over with her stick and sprinkled some more water in the coals. She knew Tae's age wasn't necessarily a bad thing, but Bristol had mentioned she was taking her in partly because she had gotten into some trouble at school in the first few weeks of the academic year. Tae had been through a lot, and Jan knew it was a good thing that she was making friends. But still, Tae wasn't exactly the kind of kid Jan had had in mind when she'd encouraged her granddaughter to get more involved in youth group.

"She seems like a nice girl," Jan said.

Tommy nodded. "Avery will be a good influence on her."

Jan forced herself to smile. As long as Avery influenced Tae and not the other way around. But Avery had a good head on her shoulders.

Jan looked over at the crowd of kids moving toward the rustic restroom down the path in the dim light. She saw that Avery was currently trying to balance her flashlight on her nose. Well, her granddaughter had a good head on her shoulders most of the time.

"Justin, put that stick down!" Tommy bolted up just in time to stop one kid from ramming another with a pointy stick. Jan felt suddenly weary. Had junior high kids always been this challenging, or was she losing patience as she got older? She turned the coals over one more time, and then pushed herself up. Then she went over to the tent she was sharing with Avery, grabbed her toiletries kit, and trudged down the dirt path toward the restroom. The little cinderblock building was dim and crowded with preteen girls shrieking and dancing, but Jan brushed her teeth and headed back toward the tent. She kept her flashlight trained on the patch of dirt in front of her, and out of the corner of her eye, she saw something come flying out at her.

"Hey Grandma—"

Jan's heart just about stopped. "Goodness, Avery. Don't jump out at me like that." Jan wasn't sure what she had been expecting. Sure, the forest on either side of the path was full of all kinds of creatures. This was Maine, after all, and everything from raccoons to moose could be roaming this forest. But most wildlife didn't carry flashlights. Jan put her hand up to block the light.

"Sorry, Grandma." But the girl didn't look sorry. She looked like she was up to something. "Hey, can I sleep in Tae's tent? She has an extra place in hers."

"I'm afraid not. I'll be lonely in my tent without you."

"I'll just be a few feet away in another tent. Please?"

Jan knew she couldn't let herself be hurt by Avery's question. She was the one who had wanted Avery to make friends. Still, she had to admit it stung a bit.

"You'll see her in the in the morning," Jan said calmly.

Avery stuck out her lower lip, but then she said "Fine" and ran off.

A few minutes later, Jan was snuggled into her sleeping bag and Avery was settling down beside her. Jan pulled up the quilt she'd layered over the sleeping bag. It felt snug and cozy inside their little domed tent, and Jan felt herself relax a bit. Sure, she could hear giggling and every whispered word in each of the nylon tents set up mere feet away, but she and Avery were safe and snug in here. She looked over and saw that Avery was staring at something under her sleeping bag. A soft splash of light was coming up out of the bag.

"It's time to put the phone away, Avery," Jan said. She tried to keep the frustration out of her voice. She didn't understand why the kids all seemed to have brought cell phones along for one night in the woods. Who did they think they were going to need to call?

"Fi-ine." Avery turned the phone off and rolled over in her sleeping bag. Suddenly, the tent was dark, and even with the rustling of sleeping bags and whispers of the kids in other tents and the faint noises of voices coming from other campsites, it only took a few minutes before Jan was sound asleep.

WHEN JAN WOKE up, weak sunlight was starting to stream into the tent. Against all odds, she'd slept deeply, and she felt refreshed as she opened her eyes. Refreshed but sore. Goodness. Had the ground gotten harder or was she getting softer? She rolled over, and saw that Avery's sleeping bag was empty. She jolted awake.

Where was Avery? Logically, Jan knew that she'd probably just gone to the bathroom or something innocuous, but she still couldn't help the jolt of fear that coursed through her. Jan unzipped the tent and poked her head out. Goodness. It was chilly out here. Inside the tent the air had stayed warmer, but out here she could see her breath. It definitely felt like the week before Thanksgiving.

"Avery?" Jan whispered. She scanned the campsite. The tents were set up in a circle around the perimeter of the campsite, and though she heard some movement in some of them, it was mostly still.

She didn't see Avery. Her backpack was gone and her shoes were not outside the door where she'd left them last night. Jan headed back into the tent and pulled on a fleece and a hat, and then she pulled her boots on and stepped out of the tent. It felt good to stretch, and she looked around the small campsite, but didn't see any movement. She would check the restroom. Jan grabbed her toiletries and headed down the path, but the bathroom was empty, save for the spiders in the corners that were now clearly illuminated in the morning light.

Where could she be? Jan tried not to panic. Avery hadn't just vanished in the night. She hadn't been eaten by a bear or carried off by a moose. Jan would have heard that. She had to be around here somewhere. Jan headed back to the tent, looking around as she walked, but there wasn't anyone else on the path.

Jan climbed back into the tent and looked around. Avery's phone was gone too, but the rest of her things were still here. What time was it anyway? Jan pulled out her phone to check the time and saw that it was just past seven a.m. There was a message from Bob, her fiancé. She still got excited thinking about that word. After many ups and downs, Bob had surprised Jan with a brilliant-cut diamond ring and the news that he'd bought the Victorian house across the street from Tea for Two, the tearoom she ran with her cousin Elaine. Jan read Bob's message: *Having a good time with Barb. She says hi. I miss you and will see you soon.*

Bob's sister Barb had lost her husband earlier this year, and Bob had gone to visit her in Texas for the week. Jan was disappointed that she wouldn't get to spend the Thanksgiving holiday with her fiancé, but she understood that Bob felt the need to be with his sister during this time.

I miss you too. Hope you have a great day, Jan texted back.

And—oh wait. There was also a text message from Avery. *I'm going with Tae to find the waterfall.*

Sent at 6:15 a.m.

Well. You couldn't get this girl out of bed before ten on a regular Saturday morning, but bring her to the woods, and she's up and ready to hike at 6:15? Jan shook her head.

She wasn't sure where the waterfall was, but she knew the whole group was supposed to hike to it later this morning. It was only supposed to be a mile or so away. Why couldn't the girls have waited to go with everyone else? Why the urgent need to go ahead of the group? Jan knew there were no answers to these questions. They were thirteen and fourteen. There was no discernible logic to what they did.

Jan's first instinct was to rush out after the girls and find them and drag them back, accompanied by a stern lecture about wandering off into the woods alone. But no doubt by the time she caught up with them, they'd be nearly back anyway. She sighed and unzipped the tent again. As soon as they smelled breakfast cooking, they'd no doubt come running. In the meantime, she would get the camp stove started and get water for coffee and tea going.

Yes, tea. That would help. After a nice hot cup of Earl Grey, this wouldn't seem like such a big deal. She grabbed her travel mug and zipped the tent back up. But as she made her way over to the makeshift camp kitchen, she couldn't help the uneasy feeling in her gut.

FROM THE
GUIDEPOSTS ARCHIVES

This story, by Judy Tipton Rush of Little Rock, Arkansas, originally appeared in *Guideposts*.

Strokes don't hurt. At least, mine didn't. I woke up one bright June morning in 1999 to the sound of the radio and the smell of the bacon my husband, Ed, was frying in the kitchen. I felt a little groggy, but not much worse than I usually do before my first cup of coffee. I threw off the big warm handmade quilt, pulled on my robe and went downstairs. Just as I stepped into the kitchen, the phone rang. I grabbed it before Ed could answer.

"Hello?" I said, trying to sound cheerful. But something else came out. Was that my voice? The word sounded strange, garbled. Maybe I was still dreaming.

"Judy?" the person on the other end asked, apparently as confused as I was. "Is that you?" I opened my mouth to answer. I couldn't. I turned to Ed, trying to call for help. Like in a nightmare, my lips moved, but no words came out.

Ed rushed me to the hospital. I collapsed in the emergency room.

I hadn't been dreaming, the doctor informed me. I'd had a stroke, and there would be some damage.

"It could've been much worse," the doctor tried to reassure me. "Because Ed got you here so quickly, you have a good chance of recovering. It'll take time and physical therapy, but you should consider yourself lucky. Very lucky."

Lucky? I thought. Right.

I was the self-sufficient, independent type, the girl who could type 65 words a minute without making a single mistake and crack a joke or tell a story with the best of them. Our house was decorated with my watercolors. My hand-sewn quilts had won prizes and had been exhibited at shows around the world.

Inside, I felt the same as ever, raring to go. But outside—what a difference! I'd lost all power of speech. I couldn't use my right arm or my right leg at all. Yes, physical therapy was my best hope. But my progress was slow. I had to learn to walk again, step by step, like a toddler. I had to learn to speak again, using word association to remember even simple words. If I forgot the word apple, for instance, I'd repeat fruit, round, color, red over and over until it stuck in my mind.

At six months my right foot continued to drag like a ball and chain. I constantly had to stop mid-sentence to grope for words. It was maddening. After a year of therapy, I couldn't even grocery shop on my own. It was still a struggle to do things like dial a phone number or send an e-mail. Never mind quilting.

"Judy, you're not going to get better overnight," Ed reminded me. "You have to be patient."

Turning the Tables

I knew that recovery took time. It was just that I expected to have made more progress by this point. *I've been working so hard in therapy, Lord. I have been patient, haven't I?*

My physical therapist recommended needlework to improve my fine motor skills. Why not give cross-stitch a try? I loved sewing and quilting. Still, Ed had to thread the needle for me. That was annoying. Then I couldn't get the darn thing to do what I wanted. I ended up with a mess of chaotic lines. I pricked my fingers so many times I felt like a pincushion. I threw the square in the trash.

One day my friend Sharon dropped by. "How's the needlework going?" she asked. Sharon and I belonged to the same quilt guild. A lot of my friends were members, and I really missed our meetings. Not just the quilting, but all the gabbing.

"Just fine," I said, tight-lipped.

"Maybe you can start quilting again," she went on. "I'm using one of those computerized sewing machines now. It's amazing! They perform so much better than the old ones. You should see. There's going to be a quilt festival in Houston in a few months. Why don't you come along with me?"

I stole a glance at my useless hands. "Maybe," I told Sharon. "But I don't think so."

I couldn't get Sharon's invitation to the quilt festival out of my head. But I had to admit, the thought of going all the way to Houston scared me. I still had trouble telling my left from my right. How could I make my way through an airport or navigate a strange city? It would be nice to see those quilts, though...

I told Ed what was on my mind.

"You should go," he urged me. "No question about it."

"But I don't even know if I'll ever be able to quilt again."

"You'll never know if you don't try," he replied.

The next time Sharon stopped by, I got up my courage and said I'd go.

I was a little worried about the plane trip to Houston. How would I be able to keep up a conversation, even with a good friend, for that long? My words came haltingly, but the more Sharon and I joked and talked, the easier it seemed to be for me to communicate. Before I knew it, we were landing in Houston.

"Chatting with you is some kind of speech therapy," I told Sharon.

At the festival, every wall was decorated with unbelievable quilts. Designs so intricate I hadn't known that you could make them with a machine. At least, not with any machine I'd ever had. I just stared at them. Each quilt was more amazing than the next.

"These are stunning," I said to Sharon. "Think of how much time it must take to make one of them."

"And how much patience," she said.

That word. Suddenly, I saw those quilts in a different light. They hadn't come together in a moment. Someone had worked at them, day by day, step by step, stitch by stitch. The way God was working on me, a little at a time. The message couldn't have been clearer: Just look what you can do with a little patience. *Thank you, Lord, for being patient with me.*

Soon as I got home, I told Ed all about the quilts at the festival.

"You know what, Judy?" he said. "You need to get one of those computerized sewing machines."

"But they're so expensive."

"We can swing it," Ed insisted. "I haven't seen you this excited about something in ages. You just talked for fifteen minutes without once pausing for a word. I think quilting would do you a world of good."

We went to Memphis a few days later and picked up a new computerized sewing machine. That evening I set to work. I decided to start with a cat pattern I'd designed myself. The moment I turned on the machine and guided the fabric through, I felt the difference. It was smoother, more precise. Even with my shaky hands, it was easy to follow patterns. I worked on the quilt late into the night. I was back at it first thing the next morning. When I finally finished that first quilt, I stretched it out on the floor in the living room. Then I called Ed in.

"What do you think?" I asked excitedly. He stared at it for a few minutes.

"I think it's just as good as anything you did before the stroke," he said. Then he smiled. "In fact, I think it's even better."

Since then, I have made dozens of quilts—all sorts of patterns, from flowers to moons and stars. Sharon and I have joined a new quilting group we call the Knot Crazies. We meet once a month. The talking plays as much a part in my recovery as the quilting. I can speak clearly now and do everyday tasks on my own.

The big things, like quilting—and healing—take more. More help. More time. More patience. But believe me, they're worth the wait.

A NOTE FROM THE EDITORS

We hope you enjoyed Tearoom Mysteries, published by the Books and Inspirational Media Division of Guideposts, a nonprofit organization that touches millions of lives every day through products and services that inspire, encourage, help you grow in your faith, and celebrate God's love.

Thank you for making a difference with your purchase of this book, which helps fund our many outreach programs to military personnel, prisons, hospitals, nursing homes, and educational institutions.

We also create many useful and uplifting online resources. Visit Guideposts.org to read true stories of hope and inspiration, access OurPrayer network, sign up for free newsletters, download free e-books, join our Facebook community, and follow our stimulating blogs.

To learn about other Guideposts publications, including the best-selling devotional *Daily Guideposts*, go to Guideposts.org/Shop, call (800) 932-2145, or write to Guideposts, PO Box 5815, Harlan, Iowa 51593.

Sign up for the Guideposts Fiction Newsletter
and stay up-to-date on the books you love!

You'll get sneak peeks of new releases, recommendations from other Guideposts readers, and special offers just for you...
and it's FREE!

Just go to Guideposts.org/Newsletters today to sign up.

Guideposts®

Visit Guideposts.org/Shop
or call (800) 932-2145

Find more inspiring fiction in these best-loved Guideposts series!

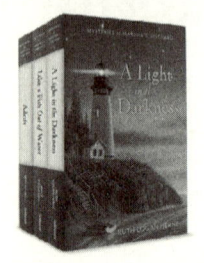

Mysteries of Martha's Vineyard
Come to the shores of this quaint and historic island and dig in to a cozy mystery. When a recent widow inherits a lighthouse just off the coast of Massachusetts, she finds exciting adventures, new friends, and renewed hope.

Tearoom Mysteries
Mix one stately Victorian home, a charming lakeside town in Maine, and two adventurous cousins with a passion for tea and hospitality. Add a large scoop of intriguing mystery and sprinkle generously with faith, family, and friends, and you have the recipe for Tearoom Mysteries.

Sugarcreek Amish Mysteries
Be intrigued by the suspense and joyful "aha!" moments in these delightful stories. Each book in the series brings together two women of vastly different backgrounds and traditions, who realize there's much more to the "simple life" than meets the eye.

Mysteries of Silver Peak
Escape to the historic mining town of Silver Peak, Colorado, and discover how one woman's love of antiques helps her solve mysteries buried deep in the town's checkered past.

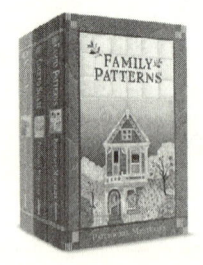

Patchwork Mysteries
Discover that life's little mysteries often have a common thread in a series where every novel contains an intriguing whodunit centered around a quilt located in a beautiful New England town.

To learn more about these books, visit Guideposts.org/Shop